Murders and Mysteries
from the
North York Moors

Peter N. Walker is the author of a number of highly successful thrillers. As Nicholas Rhea, he has written *Portrait of the North York Moors* in addition to the popular 'Constable' series.

He recently retired as an Inspector with the North Yorkshire Police to concentrate on his writing. He is married with four adult children and lives in Ampleforth.

Murders and Mysteries
from the
North York Moors

PETER N. WALKER

ROBERT HALE · LONDON

© Peter N. Walker 1988
First published in Great Britain 1988

Robert Hale Limited
Clerkenwell House
Clerkenwell Green
London EC1R 0HT

British Library Cataloguing in Publication Data

Walker, Peter N. (Peter Norman), *1936–*
    Murders and mysteries from the North
    York Moors.
    1. North Yorkshire. North York Moors.
    Mysteries
    I. Title
    001.9′4′0942846

ISBN 0-7090-3510-1

Photoset in North Wales by
Derek Doyle & Associates, Mold, Clwyd.
Printed in Great Britain by
St Edmundsbury Press Ltd, Bury St Edmunds, Suffolk.
Bound by Woolnough Bookbinding Limited.

Contents

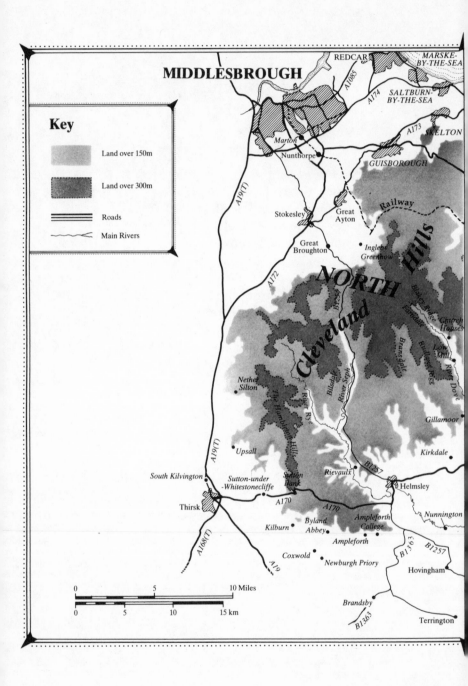

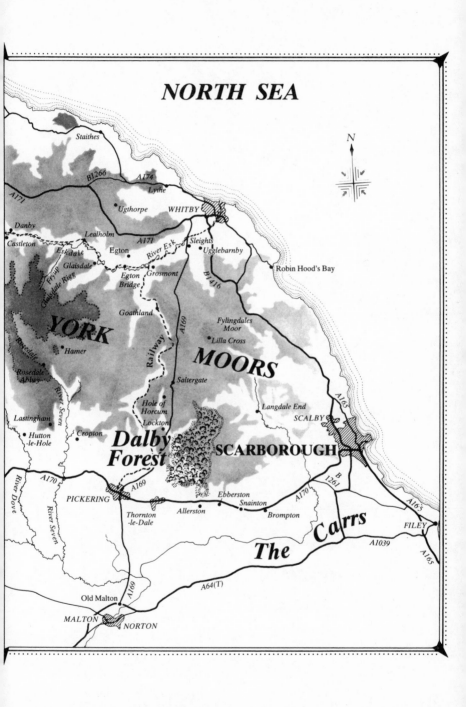

Author's Preface

It is said that all the best stories survive because they are worthy of repetition by successive generations of people. In this modest volume, I have attempted to place on record some of the more enduring tales, both ancient and modern, which have their origins in the North York Moors. Many of these stories continue to be told either verbally or in print, and will continue to be related in future years.

I have eliminated many which are pure legend, but have included some from which legends have subsequently arisen, especially the story of Sarkless Kitty (Chapter 3), the witchcraft tales (Chapter 6) and the planting of Whitby's Penny Hedge (Chapter 7, see p.103). The reader will make his or her own judgement about these yarns.

This collection of stories does embrace a long period of history, but in every one there is an element of mystery, in some cases together with a strong criminal background. Although the North York Moors are not troubled with a high rate of murder or serious crime, I have included some, and probably all, of the unsolved murders which have occurred in and around this beautiful and remote corner of North Yorkshire.

Painful though it was to include the harrowing account of the murders of two policemen, both of whom I taught and knew well, and the subsequent hunt for their killer in Dalby Forest (Chapter 10), I felt this chapter could not be omitted. It has become part of the criminal history of

England and it is an enduring tribute to the dedication and bravery of all police officers.

Much of the information in this book comes from my own files and records. In half a century of living here, and after more than twenty-five years of writing about the people, the culture, history, folklore, dialect, wildlife and topography of the North York Moors, I have amassed a huge collection of facts and information, some of which is distilled within these pages.

Having also served for thirty years in the North Riding Constabulary and subsequently the North Yorkshire Police, latterly as the Press and Public Relations Officer, I was associated with many serious crimes and murders from the viewpoint of the press, radio and television. Fortunately, very few murders have occurred within the area embraced by the North York Moors and so it remains a place of Yorkshire calm within a very turbulent Britain.

In compiling this book, I would like to thank both the Cleveland Constabulary and the North Yorkshire Police for their help, and also the staff of the Cleveland County Library at Stockton-on-Tees and Middlesbrough.

In the latter case, when I visited the Library at Middlesbrough in 1987 to research the murder of the Middlesbrough taxi-driver, Edwin Youll, another mystery was created. Someone had stolen the relevant file ...

PETER N. WALKER
1988

1   A Miscellany of Mysteries

The area known as the North York Moors comprises a tract of high ground between Middlesbrough to the north and York to the south. The market towns of Northallerton and Thirsk lie over to the west while the dramatic Yorkshire coast marks the eastern boundary. The coastal area is well known due to resorts like Scarborough and Whitby, and through the romantic fishing villages of Staithes, Runswick Bay and Robin Hood's Bay. Somewhat less well known is the range of deep dales and elevated, bleak moorland which lies between those points. There are lonely farmhouses and isolated villages, sparkling rivers and a wealth of wildlife surrounded by market-towns where the quality of life continues to be the envy of many. It is a part of England which is separated from the Yorkshire Dales and Pennines by the huge Vale of Mowbray and which even now remains largely undiscovered, probably because of its distance from the main railways, roads and centres of industry and population.

The area collectively known as the North York Moors comprises an assemblage of many smaller moors divided from one another by steep-sided dales, some of outstanding charm and beauty. It was the beauty of the area which led to its declaration, in 1952, as a National Park. Now known as the North York Moors National Park, it covers some 553 square miles (1,432 square kilometres) and is one of two National Parks within the County of North Yorkshire. The other is the Dales National Park which includes the Yorkshire Dales and the Pennine region.

Lying immediately to the south of the North York Moors National Park is a recently designated area of Outstanding Natural Beauty. This is the Howardian Hills which includes parts of Ryedale and borders some fine market towns such as Helmsley, Kirkbymoorside, Pickering and Malton while embracing the renowned Castle Howard, made so famous by the television series *Brideshead Revisited*.

The whole of the North York Moors is steeped in history and tradition. For example, out of thirty-one manorial courts still surviving in England and Wales, five are within North Yorkshire and four of them are within the North York Moors, all actively carrying out their functions, many of which relate to common land, grazing rights or rights of way.

In Eskdale, the Glaisdale and Lealholm Society for the Prosecution of Felons also survives. In the Middle Ages, societies of this kind existed to help the parish constable deal with local crime, and they were created when villagers formed themselves into associations for self-protection. They built up their finances from rewards for the recovery of stolen livestock, but as the modern police service gained acceptance and rural constables were posted to villages, these societies disappeared. The one at Glaisdale may be the only such survivor in England and Wales.

Also in Eskdale, at Egton Bridge, there is an annual Gooseberry Show where giant gooseberries are shown, and still further down the valley, a steam railway runs across the moors to Pickering and makes use of a route pioneered in the 1830s by George Stephenson. Their survival is some indication of the continuing fascination of life upon these moors.

The North York Moors contain England's largest expanse of open heather and some of its most dramatic and beautiful countryside. It is known for its legends and folklore, its adherence to centuries of custom and its long and fascinating history. There is a wealth of castles and ruined abbeys, ancient churches and delightful village inns. It is an area which containes its own mysteries, some of which have become folk-tales, but it is not known for its association with serious or unsolved crimes.

At the western side of the massive county of North Yorkshire, the Yorkshire Dales and Pennine moorlands have had their share of involvement in major criminal investigations. These cases have included the now infamous Yorkshire Ripper, the Moors Murders and the Black Panther series of crimes, but they did not occur remotely near the North York Moors – they were in a completely different part of Yorkshire. Though it cannot be denied that crime is committed within the North York Moors, much of it is minor by nature, consequently a book of this kind cannot be filled with stories of dark, murderous deeds or unsolved mysteries. This is, therefore, a mixed collection of moorland mysteries and true crime.

There are many minor mysteries, however; for example, who are the seven seamen buried in the churchyard of St Oswald's parish church at Lythe, near Whitby? During the 1914-18 War their bodies were washed onto the shore below this fine old church, among whose early priests was John Fisher. He was to become St John Fisher after his stand against Henry VIII's Reformation. But in spite of widespread enquiries in Britain and overseas, the sailors have never been indentified. They are remembered upon the war memorial which stands beside the church.

Where is the burial place of St Cedd? Is it within Lastingham church or Kirkdale Minster, both of which date to the seventh century and are only some four miles apart in the pretty Ryedale countryside.

Cedd came to Lastingham in AD 654 to found a monastery, probably the earliest in Yorkshire. He died in

AD 664. He was buried in the open air, but later a stone church was built and he was interred to the right of its altar. This might have been at Lastingham where an ancient crypt exists below St Mary's Church, but a rival claim is made by the little Minster at Kirkdale which was built around the same time. Two gravestones stand loose inside this old church, and one used to carry an inscription to the memory of King Ethelwald; it was he who asked Cedd to build the monastery at Lastingham. Could the second tombstone have been dedicated to Cedd? The inscription has gone, but there is a tale that in AD 866 as the Danes were ransacking local churches, the remains of Ethelwald and Cedd were removed from Lastingham to Kirkdale for safekeeping. So which of these quiet little churches now contains the remains of this famous English saint?

And where is Robin Hood's Cave? Years ago, there was a rumour that, deep within Arncliffe Woods between Egton Bridge and Glaisdale and overlooking the River Esk, there was a large cave used by Robin Hood and his Merry Men. It was said they sheltered here when they were evading those who hunted him, and an unlikely extension of this story was that an underground tunnel linked the cave with another at Robin Hood's Bay. I have dismissed the tunnel legend as mere fantasy, but searched without success for any sign of that cave. Is this also fantasy?

There is another curious puzzle on a six-foot-tall stone pillar at Nether Silton in the hills above Thirsk. In a field overlooked by the church and the old manor house, there are rows of initials and the date AD 1765. The letters are:

HTGOMHS
TBBWOTGWWG
TWATEWAHH
ATCLABWHEY
AD 1765
AWPSAYAA

They are said to mean, 'Here the grand old manor house stood; the black beams were oak, the great walls were good; the walls at the east wing are hidden here; a thatched cottage like a barn was here erected year AD 1765; a wide porch spans a yard and alcove.' But why erect this post and carve it with such a curious message?

Another puzzle stands by the side of the Brandsby-to-Terrington Road, not far from Dalby to the south of the moors. This used to be an old drover's road and cut into the turf on the verge is what looks like a massive fingerprint which is some twelve feet across. It is surrounded by a neat white wooden rail and is probably a relic of a game called The City of Troy. Mazes of this kind have appeared in various parts of England, but few survive today. They have had names like Julian's Bower, Robin Hood's Race, Walls of Troy or Shepherd's Ring.

This North Yorkshire example probably got its name from Trojeberg, for similar mazes have been known in Scandinavia. It seems Shakespeare referred to a game called City of Troy in *A Midsummer Night's Dream* which he wrote in 1594, although experts do not believe this maze dates to his time. It may have appeared in its present form as recently as 1900. One suggestion is that it replaced a similar one made in 1860 which had been copied from a carving on a nearby barn door. A local custom is to walk clockwise around the ridges nine times while making a wish. This ritual might have come from a religious or superstitious source, or it might have been utilized as a mysterious means of effecting cures for ailments and diseases.

But no one really knows.

A far more dramatic event occurred at a location still known as Shaw End. This lies above Lealholm in Eskdale on the path of a minor road which leads across the moors via Glaisdale Rigg and into Rosedale. Shaw End is marked by crossroads, one of which goes into Glaisdale, one into Fryup, and the others into Rosedale and Lealholm.

In 1871, a farmhouse stood near these crossroads; it was called Shaw End and during that year, or the one that followed, a terrible thunderstorm occurred one Saturday night. As dawn broke on Sunday morning, the local people were horrified to discover that lonely Shaw End House had been obliterated as if by an explosion. Only the charred remains of the house were left.

Fragments of lead window-frames were found hundreds of yards away, the stones of the house walls were scattered far and wide, the old metal oven from the kitchen was twisted into an almost unrecognizable shape while every scrap of combustible material, including timber, furniture and household goods, was burnt to nothing. But what of the occupants?

A farmer, his wife and young son lived here, and there was no sign of them. A search was therefore organized and it was soon evident that at least two bodies had been cremated. Grim, discoloured patches on the stone flags of the ground-floor bedroom indicated where they had been consumed by the inferno. But it was known that the little boy, aged five or six, also slept in that room with his parents, and there was no sign of him.

In a forlorn hope that he had avoided certain death, a man called Robert Hick began to search the remains of the outbuildings and there he found a pile of old sacks, a feature of such outbuildings. By chance, he lifted the top off the heap and there, to his surprise, was the little boy, sleeping soundly. He had escaped unscathed. The boy could not say how he had escaped the blast nor could he say what had happened to his parents or the house. Mr Hicks decided to look after the child and brought him up as his own.

But what had happened at Shaw End that awful night? It was probably a thunderbolt, but no one knows.

So far as crime is concerned, however, there are at least two unsolved criminal mysteries at lonely wayside inns upon the moors, and here it is fitting to include a note that a reminder of one of our earliest recorded murders is still to be seen on the North York Moors. The crime was committed in AD 626, but the wrong man was killed.

An assassin was sent by the King of the West Saxons to kill Edwin, King of Northumbria, in a battle for control of this vast north-eastern kingdom. It stretched from the River Humber up to the Scottish border and included the North York Moors. As Edwin journeyed across Fylingdales Moor, the assassin struck with a poisoned sword, but Edwin's devoted man-servant, a Christian called Lilla, leapt between the assassin and his King. Lilla died as a result.

So impressed was Edwin that he became a Christian and he later built a fine stone church at York; that is now York Minster. To honour Lilla, a stone cross was erected on the moors where he fell and that is now called Lilla Cross. It stands upon Lilla Howe almost in the shadow of Fylingdales Ballistic Missile Early Warning Station, so bringing the ancient and the modern into stark contrast.

Through Lilla's selfless act, Edwin survived the attempt on his life and brought Christianity to these remote regions, an act which is marked by the proliferation of abbeys and churches around the moors. Lilla Cross is the Moors' oldest Christian relic, and perhaps it is also our earliest record of a murder upon these same moors.

Lilla Cross is a landmark upon those moors, standing some 959 feet above sea level. For years it served as a guide to those who trekked across the heights from Robin Hood's Bay to the remote moorland community of Saltersgate, then known as Saltergate. In medieval times, there were many tracks across these moors, many of them using Lilla Cross as a waymarker. The present route from Pickering to Whitby did not exist until 1759, this being an extension of the first road to be build in the Whitby district. The first one ran from Whitby to Saltersgate, an indication of Saltersgate's importance.

In the seventeenth and eighteenth centuries, there was a constant procession of fishermen with strings of horses and carts bearing loads of fish; they trekked to Saltersgate from Robin Hood's Bay and Whitby, the former making use of the Old Fish Road sometimes known as the Salt Road. Based on the route of an ancient medieval track, it led from the coast via John Cross Rigg, Blea Hill Beck and over the Green Swang to Lilla Howe. From there, the route crossed Lilla Rigg and then ran via Worm Sike Rigg and Loose Howe Rigg until it met the rough track which ran across the bleak moors from Whitby. Some remains of that ancient Fish Road now form footpaths but the latter part, from Lilla Howe to what is now the A169 Whitby-Pickering Moor Road, is within the restricted area embraced by the Ballistic Missile Early Warning Station at RAF Fylingdales and consequently not accessible to the general public.

But why carry loads of fish to Saltersgate which is some eight miles from the sea as the crow flies, and some twelve very tough miles by that tortuous footpath?

The reason was salt.

Until January 1825, salt was heavily taxed. An excise duty of ten shillings per bushel had been imposed in 1798, rising to fifteen shillings by 1805. It was reduced to two shillings in 1823 then abolished soon afterwards in 1825. A bushel was eight gallons, this form of measurement being used for salt, and fifteen shillings would be around a month's wages for a plough lad on a farm. Perhaps this shows the excessive nature of this tax. At its height between 1798 and 1805, there was a massive amount of salt-smuggling, with Customs and Excise officers constantly alert for smugglers, for those who traded in salt or in liquor.

Fishermen needed salt to preserve their catches, especially when they had to be transported great distances from Robin Hood's Bay and Whitby, so a brisk trade in the smuggling of salt was established. The focal point for salt smuggling in this area was a remote moorland inn called the Waggon and Horses. Built in 1648, it stood in the centre of a huge expanse of heathery wilderness at the edge of Lockton High Moor, albeit in the shelter of a steep hill below the rim of the incredible Hole of Horcum. Several ancient tracks met here and several cottages and farms surrounded the inn, but it was, and still is, noted for its solitude.

Today, that same inn stands beside the A169 Pickering-Whitby moor road and is known as the Saltersgate Inn where it acts as host for travellers of the more modern kind, although it is still occasionally cut off by snow during the winter. A photograph inside the bar gives some indication of the depth of snow that can fall here and another picture shows the inn when it was called the Waggon and Horses.

But an ancient murder mystery surrounds this lonely hostelry.

It resulted from a battle between some salt smugglers and an exciseman. The date is uncertain although it probably occurred around 1800 when the salt tax was at its highest rate and this date can be associated with another legend about the peat fire which still burns in the bar. The inn's isolated location made it the ideal place to hide large amounts of salt, and so tons of it were brought here by traders and secreted in the cellars. The beams contained rows of fish-hooks while the inn's many cupboards were used to store the salt so that it was always ready for use. It had to be kept dry so that it would run freely, so a salt-box would probably have been built into the wall near the fire. Many remote farms, cottages and inns around the North York Moors had salt-boxes built into the walls close to the fire. These were hollowed-out sandstone troughs measuring about thirty inches long by twenty-four inches high by eighteen inches deep.

A shallower trough was inverted to form the lid and a small part was cut out so that a hand could be inserted to bring out the salt. These stone containers kept the salt dry because the peat fire was never allowed to go out, and its constant heat warmed the entire wall around the fireplace.

At the Saltersgate Inn, it is said the peat fire has never been allowed to go out since 1800, when the present fireside range was built into the bar by Dobsons of Pickering. When I called in the summer of 1987, a fire of logs was smouldering in this magnificent and famous grate, although I was told that turves of peat were placed over it during the night to maintain the tradition and to keep the fire burning.

Sometime around the turn of the last century, therefore, a group of fishermen from Robin Hood's Bay had trekked across the deserted moors, bringing their loads of fish to be salted here. By this time, there was an increase in the traffic passing Saltersgate Inn because of the new road which had been built in 1759, and because of the effect of the Turnpike Acts which produced even better roads which were fit for coaches. But the fishermen travelled at night so that the darkness would shelter them, and as they approached the lonely inn, they saw no light in the window. In the south-facing wall there is a tiny window and it was here that a lighted lantern was placed to show that excisemen were around. The absence of a light meant that it was safe to continue.

And so the little party of horses and men completed their journey. However, a lone exciseman, whose name is lost to history, was lying in wait and no one knew he was there. No one had been able to warn the incoming group. The exciseman concealed himself as the fishermen arrived and he waited until he could obtain firm evidence of their illicit purpose, finally creeping down into the inn's cellars as the fish-salting was in progress. After months of investigation, he had caught the fishermen and the innkeeper in the act and had succeeded in obtaining all the proof he required.

But he was never to leave that inn, dead or alive. A tremendous fight followed, during which the exciseman was killed; whether this was done deliberately or by accident has never been determined. In the eyes of the law of that time, it would be regarded as murder. Everyone knew the penalty – it was death by hanging, usually with the body being gibbeted afterwards. The men knew that the fight between a lone man and a party of tough fishermen going about some illegal business would be regarded as murder if the authorities ever heard about it, and so they decided to cover up their crime. After all, travellers did get lost upon those moors; many lone horsemen and solitary foot travellers died and were never seen again, their bodies being left to rot among the deep heather, so who could prove that the exciseman had ever reached Saltersgate?

Confident that their crime would never be discovered, the fishermen and the innkeeper agreed upon a conspiracy of silence and decided to bury the corpse beneath the hearth which contained the old peat fire. And so it was done; their deed would never be known. Very soon afterwards, in 1800, a new fireplace was installed and that is the one which can be seen today. The exciseman is said to be buried beneath it.

Inevitably rumours began to circulate about the death of the exciseman, but they never progressed beyond the stage of being rumours. Perhaps the fishermen boasted of their perfect crime? Perhaps the locals of the Saltersgate Inn had heard the story? Maybe the installer of the new fireplace had uncovered the corpse and agreed to keep his silence? Since that time, the peat fire has never been allowed to go out, and a legend has arisen that if it does go out, the ghost of the exciseman will return to haunt the inn.

From being a smugglers' haunt, the Waggon and Horses became a noted coaching inn; a toll-gate was installed here and horses could be obtained for the Neptune and Royal Mail coaches which ran past several times a week from the 1820s.

Today, it continues to provide accommodation for travellers, many of whom sit and gaze into the historic old fireplace whose flame has burned for nearly two hundred years. But does the body of a murdered excisemen lie beneath it and if so, who killed him? No one was ever brought to justice.

Stories of suspicious deaths or even murder continue to circulate about another moorland inn where, at various times, three people are said to have died under suspicious circumstances. Sadly, the accounts of these deaths are very limited.

The inn was the Lettered Board at Hamer which occupied a desolate and lofty position between the moorland villages of Glaisdale and Rosedale. Only a windswept pile of stones and a patch of uncharacteristically smooth grass surrounded by a sea of heather remain visible as reminders of that ancient inn. It was once a thriving house where huge flocks of sheep were farmed, but those moribund relics are all that is left and they stand beside the unclassified moorland road that runs between Rosedale Abbey and Glaisdale. The ruins are not far from Hamer Bridge which is marked on Ordnance Survey maps, roughly a mile away among some long-deserted coal pits.

Surrounding the ruins is the bleak moorland, a windswept, open area thick with heather but devoid of trees, and a short distance to the north is the beautifully named Blue Wath Beck which flows from the moors to join Wheeldale Beck, the Murk Esk and eventually the River Esk. To the south, Hartoft Beck runs across the moor and into Rosedale where it joins the River Seven. This lonely pile of rubble is therefore upon the highest point of these moors, well over a thousand feet above sea level.

Today the location is known merely as Hamer, although Hamer House or Hamer Inn are names which have been used in the recent past. Most references ignore the correct name, i.e. The Lettered Board Inn, and its lonely address is variously given as Rosedale, Fryup or Hartoft. The forty-two-mile long-distance Lyke Wake Walk passes the ruins where support vehicles often wait among the stones to nourish hikers with refreshments and practical assistance. Years ago, several moorland tracks converged at this place and the main route was once a monks' trod, the local name for a footpath, linking the abbeys of Whitby and Rosedale. The precise age of the old inn is uncertain, although I would estimate it has witnessed at the very least some three centuries of severe moorland winters. From its uncertain beginnings, the inn has been the focal point for many weary travellers, while today's motorists drive past with barely a thought for this innocuous heap of stones.

It is difficult to believe that coal-mining brought men to these remote moors although evidence of the old pits is still visible near the remains of the Lettered Board. In its heyday, the farmers of Eskdale would despatch wagon-loads of coal from these pits to places in Ryedale such as Cropton, Hutton-le-Hole and Kirbymoorside, and would later return with wagon-loads of lime for their fields.

This trade, and other passing horse-drawn vehicles plying between Whitby and the south, meant that Hamer's isolated Lettered Board Inn was a very busy establishment.

There are tales of dozens of horse-drawn vehicles being assembled outside at one time, with strings of powerful horses enjoying a break as their drivers relaxed inside. The drivers always carried sacks of fresh clover for the horses, while the men enjoyed egg-and-bacon pies made by their wives, or the wives of their farmer customers, and washed them down with pints of beer from the inn.

It is said that one famous customer was Captain William Scoresby (1760-1829), the famous navigator, Arctic explorer, whaling expert and inventor of the Crow's Nest. In 1806, with his son (also called William) as chief mate, he, took a ship closer to the North Pole than any other man. The senior Scoresby was born at Cropton near Pickering, the son of a farmer, and he lived there for a while, travelling across the moors to Whitby from where he operated his highly successful whaling enterprise. He employed several men from Cropton on his whaling expeditions. Later, he had two houses in Whitby, but regularly made this trip across the moors from Whitby to Cropton. He probably came along Glaisdale Dale where even now two farms record that this was the route from Whitby to York, London and beyond. Those farms are still called York House and London House.

Hamer's role as in inn declined after 1870, the year a local writer called Joseph Ford was born at the remote house. His father was landlord and I have a copy of a licensing application dated 1858 in which the liquor licence of the Lettered Board was transferred to Joseph Ford Senior.

The younger Joseph Ford, who died in 1944, has left behind some stories of Hamer and they provide a vivid picture of the windswept and snowbound inn. He relates how elderly travelling salesmen would trek onto these moors, even in the height of winter, to sell trinkets from bags and baskets. These were mendicants and old soldiers, and they often met their deaths on these inhospitable moorlands.

There are stories of how sheepdogs, during the spring and summer after a particularly hard winter, would find the decaying bodies or bones of these men. Bodies were found lying near the streams or other isolated places where they had fallen, unable to reach the warmth or security of Hamer or any other shelter. The weather had killed them.

One harrowing story concerns an old cork-seller. Farmers' wives and innkeepers were his main customers and Joseph Ford's mother knew this man. He died on the moor during one of these ferocious winters, and his skeleton was found very close to the inn, with his basket of corks nearby. The corks identified him to his searchers, but many who perished in similar circumstances were never identified.

But three mysteries continue to haunt Hamer. I cannot pinpoint the date of any with accuracy but believe the first mystery occurred around the latter years of the last century, probably as the inn was beginning its decline. Two men called Hicks and Atkinson travelled by horse across the moors from Whitby towards Rosedale and stopped for the night at Hamer. I do not know their business, nor the reason for them being on this road. However, they were given a room at the inn and went to bed early, each in good health and in good spirits. But the following morning, both were found to be dead. There were no signs of injury or of a struggle, and even though an inquest was held, the cause of their death was never determined.

I have one account which suggests that these deaths were an awful accident. It seems that the room in question had been newly-plastered, and that it had no chimney or fireplace, and no ventilation. Furthermore, the water in the plaster had swollen the woodwork of the door and windows, and the unfortunate guests may have suffocated through lack of air or inhaled some noxious fumes from the drying plaster.

Not long after this incident, the Lettered Board ceased to be an inn. The precise date is not certain, although there was a Lettered Board Inn at Hartoft which was licensed in 1901 and it is believed this licence continued until 1929. The house did continue as a private dwelling until late in the 1930s, the last family to live there being called Boddy. I remember the inn shortly after it was abandoned as a house, and the second mystery is a story of a murder that was committed here.

Very little is known of this crime. The victim was said to be the wife of one of the long line of licensees.

After the murder, he moved down from the moor to a cottage in an adjoining dale where I am assured his descendants still live. But I can find no formal record of this murder, nor of any legal outcome or prosecution.

The third murder, of which nothing has apparently been printed, is said to concern two wagoners who viciously fought one another in the bar of the Lettered Board. One picked up the heavy poker and savagely killed the other. Thereafter that poker was chained to the hearth so that it could be used only for tending the fire. The landlord did not want a recurrence of that fight, and the poker was still chained there within living memory. But it appears that the full circumstances of this fight have never been made public.

And it is too late now for the meagre remains of Hamer's lonely Lettered Board Inn to reveal its deepest secrets.

2   Danby – and the Hand of Glory

Danby is a very open and pleasant village of sturdy stone houses on the upper reaches of the River Esk. Nestling below the rim of the surrounding moorland, it is worthy of exploration and is sometimes called Danby-in-Cleveland to distinguish it from other villages of the same name. This full title can be misleading, however. Danby is not within the new Cleveland County but lies deep within North Yorkshire and well inside the boundaries of the North York Moors National Park. The village and its surrounding countryside were immortalized by Canon J.C. Atkinson (1814-1900), the famous vicar of Danby who wrote a classic book entitled *Forty Years on a Moorland Parish*.

There are several places of interest. High in Danby Dale, for example, not far from Canon Atkinson's church and now, his burial-place, is Botton Hall. This is the central point of a community of mentally and physically handicapped people which was established in 1955 by the Camphill Village Trust. Members of this community maintain themselves and their 'village' by making high-quality goods which are on sale to visitors. They have their own workshops, post-office, coffee-bar, social centre and shops, with outside help provided by volunteers.

At the end of Danby Dale, the village of Danby with the nearby hamlet of Ainthorpe provide a focal point for people from the outlying areas, with their railway station, village hall, shops and inns.

Danby is also the home of the Moors Centre where a wealth of information about the North York Moors and the work of the National Park Committee is available; there are books, exhibitions, a cafeteria, picnic areas and more. This attractive Moors Centre, formed within a splendid country house, has made Danby a mecca for tourists or visitors and for those who seek to learn more about this fascinating district.

In addition to its beautiful countryside, Danby has also played a small part in the nation's history. Spanning the River Esk a short distance downstream is a narrow and pretty pack-horse bridge called Duck Bridge built around 1386, and behind it is Danby Castle. Perched on the side of Danby Rigg, this was the seat of the Latimers and it is said that Catherine Parr, sixth wife of Henry VIII, once lived here. The castle is not open to the public for it is a working farm, but one of its rooms is still used by the ancient Danby Court Leet and Baron which administers rights of way and common land. It is one of only thirty-eight courts leet which survive in England and one of four within the North York Moors.

But Danby can also claim a part in the criminal history of the Moors. It is a role which is not well known and which tends to be overlooked for it forms little or no part in Danby's overall appeal to tourists and visitors. A clue can be obtained by visiting the Whitby Museum in its peaceful setting at Pannett Park, Whitby. On display there is the shrivelled and once gruesome Danby Hand of Glory. It is a genuine human hand severed from the right arm of a gibbeted criminal.

I am not sure whether this is the only surviving example of a Hand of Glory, but most certainly it is a rare relic from our comparatively recent criminal history. A Hand of Glory was a hideous charm used by burglars. It was usually the right hand which was cut from the corpse of a gibbeted man; it was pickled and then cured before being carried during their criminal raids. At the most, they believed it made them invisible; at the least, it enabled them to avoid arrest.

The name probably comes from the French *maine de glorie* which is a corruption of mandragora, the formal name of the mandrake plant whose roots were accredited by thieves with similar powers.

It is not known how the Danby Hand of Glory survived after 1820 when it was thought to have been last used, but by chance it came into the possession of an antiquarian at Danby. He kept it for many years and as he approached the end of his life, he considered burying it in Danby churchyard. Instead, he passed it to the Eskdale historian and author Joseph Ford (1870-1944) who in turn passed it to another friend, having been given an assurance that it would never be lost to posterity. Today, the Danby Hand of Glory is safe within Whitby Museum; it was taken there from a cottage at nearby Castleton, the home of Dr Chalmers.

Until the middle years of the nineteenth century, there were many Hands of Glory and they were used by burglars as they committed their crimes. Most superstitious burglars would obtain their own Hands, and the only source was the body of a criminal hanging on a gibbet. Having been cut from the dead body, the Hand was then cured in a manner I shall describe later, but this practice was not restricted to this country, nor indeed to the last century.

Hands were mankind's first tools and weapons which meant that life depended upon them. It is easy to understand why, long before the Christian era, the human hand was used as a charm against evil and why the open hand suggested power or a raised hand was later used in priests' blessings.

In the absence of real hands, models have been utilized for the purpose of bringing luck or deterring evil and some evidence of this can even be seen in the shape of modern door-knockers. Today they provide a useful function, but in the past the presence of a hand on the door was to keep away evil spirits. Diseases were thought curable by the use of hands – scrofula, otherwise known as the King's Evil, was thought capable of being cured by a touch of the King's hand while other cures have been claimed due to the laying on of hands. There are many more instances of hands or models of hands being used for superstitious or religious purposes. We need only to think of the symbol of friendship in the shaken hand, the menace of a closed fist, the welcoming sign of open hands or the joining of hands to cement a relationship.

Within the criminal world, however, the hand also had its place, more often through being cut off both as a punishment and as a deterrent. Even a writer who offended against the law could have the right hand cut off. One account dated 1581 says,

I remember, then being present, that Stubbs, a writer, when his right hand was struck off, plucked his hat with his left hand and said in a loud voice 'God Save the Queen'; the multitude standing about was deeply silent, either out of horror at this new form of punishment or out of commiseration with the man.

The punishment was not new; in 1176, Henry II ordained that the punishment for robbery, murder, false coining and arson should be amputation of the right hand and right foot, while striking a blow in a palace or court of Henry VIII was punishable by loss of the right hand. Throughout medieval times in this country and in Europe, a belief developed that the hand of a man who had been hanged, or who had committed suicide, possessed strong magical or curative powers. For this reason, gibbets and gallows were raided after a hanging, either to remove the dead hand or to touch oneself with one while it remained on the corpse. Those who suffered from goitres, wens, the king's evil, cancer and various tumours and sores, all believed that a dead hand offered a cure. Even childless women believed that a touch of a dead hand would remedy their barrenness. There is one story of a child being treated for whooping-cough by eating a slice of bread-and-butter which had been placed in the hand of a corpse.

The strength of these beliefs often meant that very nervous people trekked in secret through the darkness towards their nearest wayside gibbet. Some took ladders, and others relied on friends to help them reach the swinging hand which they then drew across the affected part, perhaps three, seven or nine times, each being a magic number.

It is not surprising, therefore, that criminals felt that they could bring good fortune to their enterprises by making use of these magic hands.

In the mind of criminals, the most powerful charm was the hand of a man hanged on the gibbet and so, over the centuries and across Europe, the Hand of Glory became an important part of the criminal's equipment. In 1588, there is an account of a trial where two alleged witches used a Hand of Glory while poisoning their victims in the belief it would prevent their capture, but it appears to have been chiefly used by burglars, some of whom thought it rendered them invisible. Most, however, believed it would permit them to go about their crimes without being caught. One of its supposed powers was to make sleeping people remain asleep and awake persons to remain awake, an ideal charm for a villain who operated at night.

It is perhaps worth mentioning at this point that the crime of burglary was classified as a felony and carried the death penalty. This penalty continued until 1837 when the death penalty was limited to cases where violence had been committed against a person during burglary, and in 1861 the penalty was reduced to penal servitude for life. Until 1967, the crime of burglary involved breaking into dwelling-houses during the night hours, a man's home being regarded as sacrosanct especially at night. Today, burglary is a much lesser crime; it is not restricted to the night-time hours nor even to dwelling-houses.

To go a-burgling before 1837, therefore, meant risking one's life, and so all burglars sought ways of reducing that risk. The Hand of Glory was one of those ways. It is interesting that its demise occurred around the time of reforms in criminal punishment and when the death penalty ceased to be utilized against convicted burglars. The last recorded use of a Hand of Glory was in 1831.

I do not know from which hanged criminal the Danby Hand of Glory came, nor do I know who used it, but its creation would have followed the traditional pattern. It would have been cut from the corpse of a man hanging on a local gibbet and from no other source. Either hand would suffice although it seems that right hands were favoured.

The Hand must be cut from the corpse as soon as possible after death, a fact which meant that most hangings were attended by criminals who were anxious to acquire a Hand. Once severed, the Hand was tightly wrapped in a shroud or a draw-sheet which was severely tightened to squeeze out the last drops of blood. The next stage was to put it through a curing or pickling process. One method was to use a solution of salt, saltpetre and pepper, all carefully powdered and it was allowed to absorb this mixture for about two weeks. This has been likened to the curing of a ham or side of bacon, a skill in which country folk excelled.

After curing, the Hand was then dried. This could be done by placing it in the sun, or by popping it into a clay receptacle for drying over the heat from burning vervain and ferns. Sometimes, the Hand was forcibly dried in an oven, but it seems this was not the correct manner. When dry, it was quite hard and ready for its awesome work as a charm.

But another part of the charm had yet to be completed.

When in use by burglars, the Hand was effectively a candle-holder, but the candle must also be fashioned from further revolting ingredients. An account by Colin de Planey in *Dictionnaire Infernal* (1818) tells us that it was made from the fat of a hanged man, virgin wax and Lapland Sesame, the latter being a kind of plant from which oil can be obtained. The wick had to be made from human hair taken from the corpse of a hanged man, although I believe some exponents made use of the hair of a dead child. The charm was made complete by the awful candle being placed between the fingers of the Hand of Glory. And, in that form, with the candle alight, the burglars went about their nefarious business.

They believed that the Hand of Glory, complete with its lighted candle, had various magical properties; it could render its owner invisible, it could paralyse anyone who set eyes upon the burning flame (except, of course, the owner), it could make sleeping people remain asleep or waking people (i.e. the criminals) remain awake. Its power was broken only when the candle was extinguished and this could be done only by pouring on milk or blood. No other liquid would extinguish the magic flame.

It follows that, for the enterprising burglar, a Hand of Glory was a formidable and much-sought-after charm. Anything that would ensure uninterrupted slumber by the residents of a wayside inn or a house during a burglary was of inestimable value. This is ample reason for burglars raiding so many gibbets and slicing off the felons' hands.

In common with most charms, however, there was a verbal ritual to complete and in this case, it was chanted as the candle was lit. Generally, a burglar would enter the intended property, sometimes with the help of an accomplice who opened doors or windows, and having thoroughly checked that everyone was asleep, he would then light the gory candle. It was essential that only the burglars were awake as the candle was lit, for as he applied the flame, he had to chant these lines:

Let those who rest more deeply sleep,
Let those awake their vigils keep;
Oh Hand of Glory, shed thy light,
Guide us to our spoils tonight.

As the weird and unearthly light filled the room, more lines were chanted:

Flash out thy blaze, oh skeleton hand
And guide the feet of our trusty band;
Let those who are awake keep awake
And those who are asleep keep asleep.

From place to place, there are slight variations in the words of these incantations but the above is the essence of the verses. The important thing was to keep the flame burning because so long as it blazed, the burglars thought the magic spell would continue.

There are several accounts of the use of the Hand of Glory during burglaries. Richard Harris Barham (1788-1845) mentions it in *The Ingoldsby Legends* and the Jesuit demonologist Del Rio tells how a thief lit a Hand of Glory before raiding a house, but was seen by a servant girl. The villains had not checked that everyone in the house was asleep before lighting the candle.

The incantation meant the servant would remain awake, so her task was to rouse the family. As the thief disappeared to ransack the house, she tried to extinguish the candle by throwing water, then beer over it and finally achieved success by using skimmed milk. The household awoke and the thief was arrested.

This is the basis of many tales surrounding the Hand of Glory, and stories of its use in North Yorkshire follow this general outline. In 1790, for example, a traveller in women's clothes arrived at the Old Spital Inn at Stainmore high on the Pennines. This location was then in the North Riding of Yorkshire. She asked to stay the night, saying she must leave very early next morning. The landlady therefore arranged for a maid to remain awake all night to ensure the guest received an early call and some breakfast.

But the alert maid noticed men's boots protruding from beneath the 'woman's' clothing and pretended to be asleep. As she produced a realistic snore, the visitor pulled a Hand of Glory from 'her' pocket, lit the candle and passed it over the maid's face while chanting:

Let those who are awake keep awake
And those who are asleep keep asleep.

He then put the Hand on the kitchen table and went to open the door of the inn, to allow his companions to enter; as he popped his head outside to whistle for them, very bravely, the maid surprised him by suddenly throwing her weight against him and managed to thrust him fully outside. She even managed to lock the door before he could turn around. The Hand remained on the table with its eerie flame filling the kitchen, and when she tried to rouse the sleeping landlord and his family, none would awake. The angry men were now trying to force the door, and then she remembered that milk would extinguish the candle. In a trice, she threw a dish of milk over the flame and after it had spluttered and died, she had no trouble rousing the family. The would-be thieves were then caught.

Use of the Hand of Glory is recorded in another case in the North Riding of Yorkshire, this time at a busy coaching inn on the Great North Road, a few miles from the western edge of the Moors. In November 1824, a month noted for its heavy snowstorms and severe winds, lots of coaches were marooned on the awful roads and their passengers were obliged to find overnight shelter at roadside inns.

One such inn was the Oak Tree on Leeming Lane which was a stretch of the Great North Road north of Boroughbridge. Leeming Lane was, and still is, a long, flat highway which follows the route of a Roman road through Leeming, Catterick and beyond to the north. It is now the A1. One night, because of an unexpected influx of travellers from the Red Rover coach which was sheltering from the appalling weather, the grooms and man-servants had to sleep in haylofts and saddle-rooms, while two maids were forced to sleep in the kitchen.

The maids, Peggy Scott and Jenny Brown, were to use a rough hammock-type of bed slung from the rafters. Supported by ropes and iron bands, it hung about three feet below the ceiling. The girls had to undress on the floor, climb onto a chair which stood on the table, and finally clamber into their makeshift bed. Once they were in bed, their mistress took away their clothes, replaced the chair on the floor and went to her own bed. From below, the girls were quite invisible.

The following is based on a contemporary account which comes from *The Hand of Glory* by Richard Blakeborough (North Yorkshire County Library at Northallerton). The maids giggled and laughed in their curious and uncomfortable bed, but sleep was far from easy. The excitement and strange bed conspired to keep them awake and then, as they tried to will themselves into slumber, they heard men's voices. Peggy placed a finger over Jenny's lips, saying, 'Sssh! Lie still, no one will find us here!'

By peeping over the side of her hammock, the glow from the dying embers of the log fire in the kitchen enabled her to see two men. She recognized them as passengers from the Red Rover and as the girls lay in uneasy silence, it became clear that the men intended to rob two horse-dealers and a wealthy merchant who were also travelling on that coach. Their intended victims were asleep upstairs, and the men also mentioned the landlord's cash-box. It would be full of cash after the evening's eating and drinking. As the terrified girls lay huddled together above the heads of the two plotters, they heard someone knock on the kitchen window.

'There's Jim with the horses,' whispered one of the plotters. 'It's time we got to work. All's still.'

At that moment, the nervous Jenny fainted. With a faint sigh, she collapsed into unconsciousness. One of the men heard her and asked, 'What's that?'

'Just the wind outside,' said his companion. 'It's blowing a full gale out there.'

Then the first man said, 'So let's get to work. I'll make sure everybody is asleep, then put the candle in the Hand.'

Peggy was horrified. She had heard awful stories of the Hand of Glory from both her mother and her grandmother and she almost fainted too, but she gritted her teeth and decided to try and prevent the burglary. She knew how to extinguish the flame and as she lay alone, she evolved a plan of action. As soon as the conspirators left the kitchen on their tour of the premises, she would drop to the floor, find a jug of milk and put out the flame. Then she would scream for all she was worth.

As the two men left to check that everyone was asleep, Peggy began her action, but she was a little too early. She dropped to the floor and padded quietly into the pantry, but the men returned; they'd merely been on a reconnaissance and had come back to activate their Hand of Glory. In the darkness, she managed to hide in an inglenook and could observe them through a crack in the panelling.

'Them what is asleep will stay asleep,' said the older man. 'Them what's awake, well, they'll get a crack on the head!'

As he spoke, he unwrapped a small package and showed the contents to his companion, saying, 'This was poor Tom's hand. I had lots of bother getting hold of it, but managed. They were watching the gibbet, you see, to stop us getting our Hands but I scared the watchers. It was a dark night and I scared 'em off, saying to myself 'It's now or never' because me and Tom had agreed that whoever

got strung up first, the other was to have his right hand.
You see, in a manner of speaking it would keep us together
in the old business. It was a friendly thought of Tom's. So
he's with us now, in this Hand.'

Peggy watched him tending the wizened hand which lay
on the table, and there was a deathly hush in the room.
Very carefully, he began to remove the wrappings from the
awful candle. At this point, Jenny moved in her makeshift
bed and they heard her.

'Hush, there's somebody up there!' said the older man,
pointing to Jenny's hammock. 'Take a look!'

The younger man placed a chair on the table, then
climbed up to inspect the strange bed which hung from the
rafters. In the dim light, he found the terrified Jenny,
hugging the blankets around her and speechless with fear.
Wide-eyed as she peered at him, her pretty face captivated
the young criminal.

He put a finger to her lips. 'Hush, lass, don't make a
sound, not one word and on my honour, no hurt will come
to you. Come down from there, bring a quilt with you. Now
be quick and be quiet … do as I say and I'll see you're all
right. Cause a fuss and I can't answer for my surly friend.'

And so he helped the frightened girl down from the bed
and the two men sat her on the chair which they had placed
on the floor. They began to gag her and tie her to the chair
when they spotted two pairs of garters lying on the settle.
The landlady had not removed them with the girls' other
clothes.

'There's two of them …' said the older man. 'Find the
other, quickly.'

'No,' said Jenny in a surprisingly firm voice. 'There's just
me, one set's mine, the other's my mistress's, she forgot to
take 'em away tonight ….'

The men believed her. Peggy sighed with silent relief for
Jenny had proved able to cope with the situation. She was
then gagged and bound to the chair, whereupon the young
highwayman suddenly kissed her on the forehead.

'Come on, fool!' snapped his companion. 'It's time to go to work.'

And he lit the horrible candle which he then placed in the fist of the Hand of Glory. It burned with a hypnotic light, half mesmerizing Peggy in her hiding-place and she watched as they carried it to a corner cupboard. They placed it inside.

Peggy believed that so long as that candle burned, the household could not be roused, and she waited as the men trudged upstairs to begin searching the bedrooms. Then she rushed into the kitchen and released Jenny, at the same time explaining her plans. Jenny had to remain silent until Peggy shouted, 'Robbers!' At that point, she must scream her loudest. Then Peggy secured a jug of milk from the dairy and poured it over the candle and the Hand. The flame turned scarlet, the fingers twitched a fraction and the candle fell to the floor, extinguished.

Peggy then crept into the parlour where the landlord was sleeping and roused him; he armed himself with a pistol and set about waking the stable lads and other servants who slept outside and in various downstairs rooms. Silently, they made their plans, and the landlord told some stable lads to creep outside and tie up the robbers' horses.

'Those horses'll fetch good money,' he said. 'You can divide it between you when we sell 'em.'

As this plot was being operated, the other servants concealed themselves in corners and passages, waiting to catch the highwaymen with their loot as they came downstairs, but outside, the burglars' lookout had noticed a stable-boy creeping among the horses. Immediately, he raised the alarm by hooting like an owl and the two men upstairs heard it. They lost no time trying to escape, but were caught as they rushed downstairs.

Peggy had no need to shout 'Robbers', but the older man was concerned only for his precious Hand of Glory. He could not believe that it had let him down in his hour of greatest need, and when he saw the Hand dripping with milk, he knew that the charm had not failed. It was their own work which had failed, and he blamed his young companion for his attentions to the pretty young Jenny.

Outside, their lookout did escape in the storm, leaving two horses which could be sold. When the passengers heard about the night's events, they were delighted and organized a collection among themselves for Peggy and Jenny.

This was probably the last occasion the Hand of Glory was used in the North Riding of Yorkshire, although it was used as late as 1831 in Ireland and this time it was a failure. On 3 January that year, thieves tried to ransack the home of a Mr Napier at Loughcrew in County Meath. As they entered his house, they carried a Hand of Glory in the firm belief that it would exercise power over the sleeping residents.

But it did not. Mr Napier awoke and the burglars fled, leaving the Hand behind. I have no record of its current whereabouts.

In France, there is a later record of a Hand of Glory. It was cut from the murderer Lacenaire after his execution in Paris in 1836, and was possessed by the author Maxime du Camp.

3 Farndale – Valley of Tragedy

Farndale is a remote and steep-sided valley whose wild and rugged head lies in the depths of the North York Moors. It extends for some ten miles to the north of Kirkbymoorside and it is divided by the pretty River Dove which eventually joins the River Rye. Two access roads lead into Farndale from the elevated Hutton-le-Hole to Castleton road; one is close to Hutton-le-Hole, a village known for its beauty and the thriving Ryedale Folk Museum. The other dips steeply from the same road nearer Castleton, not far from the isolated Lion Inn at Blakey, and this route requires strong nerves and good brakes. Yet another vehicular approach is through the village of Gillamoor and this offers a drive or even a walk down Surprise View which provides a panoramic view of the lower area of Farndale. Winding tracks and footpaths provide other pedestrian access points.

There is no village named Farndale. The valley comprises the hamlets of Church Houses, Low Mill and Lowna; these are some distance apart and there is a scattering of farmhouses and cottages between as they dot the slopes and valley floor. Farndale is noted, among other things, for its cruck houses and thatched cottages, many of which survived well into the 1970s. Even now, one or two remain and the general area of Ryedale, into which Farndale emerges, continues to boast an interesting collection of thatched buildings, many of which are beautifully maintained.

It is true that Farndale remains unspoilt and in many ways, it offers an echo of the past. Perhaps its unspoilt and somewhat romantic survival owes as much to a wild flower as to its splendid scenic assets. That flower is the wild daffodil. Although Farndale's name may come from the Gaelic *fearna*, which has links with the alder trees flourishing along the banks of River Dove, it is the tiny yellow daffodil which has made Farndale so popular in the spring.

Millions of them grow along the river-banks and extend six or seven miles into the dale. There are other flowers but none compares with the sheer volume of daffodils. There are several varieties and these are the true wild daffodils which are native to Britain. Rumour suggests they were introduced either by the monks of Rievaulx Abbey who once owned the land, or by the Egton Bridge martyr, Father Nicholas Postgate (*see p.71*) who planted daffodils around his home and, as some stories suggest, at other venues during his travels. But the truth is that the low-lying damp pastures of Farndale with their sandy loam soil provide precisely the right elements for their growth. They grow in other nearby moorland dales too, but not in such profusion.

Yorkshire folk call them Lenten Lilies because they bloom around Easter and Lent. Today, the Farndale daffodils are protected by law and picking the flowers or lifting the bulbs is forbidden; indeed, in 1953 the North Riding County Council designated 2,000 acres of Farndale as a local nature reserve.

Every Easter, therefore, thousands of visitors pour into this pretty dale with its steep and narrow roads. A one-way traffic system is temporarily implemented to ensure the movement of vehicles and pedestrians, but the best of the daffodils cannot be seen from a car. The finest method is to walk along the well-marked footpaths. Indeed, the whole of Farndale is ideal for hiking or rambling.

But as the visitors tour the famous flowers and walk beside the rippling stream, how many, I wonder, are aware of the mysteries which survive in this dramatic North Yorkshire valley?

The very remoteness of Farndale, especially over the earlier years of its history and indeed into the beginning of this century, has created a host of myths and legends. The valley is rich with tales of witches and hobs and is replete with superstition and folklore. Local names reflect this – between Lowna and Low Mill there is a lofty tumulus called Obtrusch, a local dialect name which means hobgoblin's leap, and I am told that flints found on the moors are still called elf darts.

In a dale with so many stories and with such a strong folk memory of witches, hobs, goblins and evil spirits, it is difficult to separate fact from fiction. But two genuine mysteries do remain. Each has, in its own way, become a legend but beneath those legends are grains of truth. The best known has become the legend of Sarkless Kitty with a ghost added for good measure, but the real girl featured in this sad story was Kitty Garthwaite.

Kitty Garthwaite was a Farndale girl. She was born towards the end of the eighteenth century, probably around 1767. Her parental home was a small and very basic thatched cottage on the southerly slopes of Rudland Rigg, just off Harland Moor. With an earthen floor and walls of local stone, it would provide the very barest of home comforts. No trace of the cottage remains. There is no record of her family circumstances and we do not know how her father earned his living. He would probably have been a craftsman or labourer working on a large farm in the area and ekeing out his living by collecting ling cowls from a burnt swizzen (burnt heather stems from an area of moor cleared by burning). These would be used on his cottage fire, or perhaps he would cut peat from the moors above his cottage by using his specially-made turf spade and knappers.

We know nothing of Kitty's younger days either, nor whether she had any brothers or sisters. It is beyond doubt, however, that she was brought up in the traditional manner of village girls, being taught at home and being shown by her mother how to run a house, to cook, sew and mend clothes, to tend livestock such as hens or geese or even larger animals like sheep, pigs, horses and cows. She was required to learn all the varied skills necessary for a woman of her time. Many girls of that era sought work 'in service'; this meant they secured posts within the larger houses or on farms, working either as milkmaids or as domestic helpers about the house or in the kitchen.

It was a secure job and many girls 'lived in' at their place of work, going home only at Martinmas and continuing with the same employer until they married. Martinmas is the Feast of St Martin of Tours which occurs on 11 November and in those times, it presented a week's holiday for the girls and boys who were working on farms. In some areas, Martinmas was celebrated on 23 November, a relic of the time before England accepted Pope Gregory's 1582 changes to the calendar; England finally accepted those changes in 1752, a few years before Kitty Garthwaite was born. But traditionalists then, and even well into this century, refused to change the dates of their important festivals. And so they celebrated Martinmas on 23 November; this would have been the 11th in the old days.

At Martinmas, therefore, whether celebrated on the old or the new date, the farm workers would return to their homes to decide whether or not they wanted to go back to the employer for whom they had worked during the past year. If not, they could attend the Martinmas Hiring Fairs in the hope they would be selected by someone else. The first day was taken up with the selection of workers, and this was followed by a week of fun, the only holiday in the year. There were stalls, food, drink, games, contests and dancing after the farmers and their wives had examined potential employees. Those who had decided to return to their former place of work had a holiday too and went along to join the fun.

Anxious to get work as a domestic servant at a farm, Kitty attended the Hirings at Kirkbymoorside in November, 1783; it was a long walk and she left home at half-past six that Wednesday morning to cover the four hilly miles. She was sixteen, a very beautiful girl with the dark hair and clear skin of the moorland people. Stockily-built and well-shod for her trek, she trudged down the dale in the chill of that November morning. She wore a new dress, made with her own hands under the skilled guidance of her mother, with a warm cape over the top, thick woollen gloves and a woolly bonnet to complete her ensemble.

She must have wondered what lay in store for her. Romances did blossom during the Hiring Fairs; young people met one another, fell in love and secured employment at the same farm. In some cases, marriages resulted. Kitty had no steady boyfriend; true, she'd been friendly with some of the lads from Farndale, for she was a very attractive girl with what would today be described as a magnetic personality. Boys instantly warmed towards this pretty girl from the edge of Harland Moor. At the Hiring Fair, she would have no trouble creating interest among both prospective employees and lads seeking romance.

This was the case. As she mingled with the crowd, chatting to those she knew and seeking someone who would give her work, she met Herbert Longster. Herbert, a fine seventeen-year-old lad, had not come seeking work; he had come for the fun of the fair, for he worked on his father's farm. This was a fine spread near Lowna which had been passed down through generations of Longsters. One day, it would belong to Herbert, and then to his son ....

Herbert Longster was a charmer and in no time, he was displaying his skills at tossing the sheaf, wrestling, running and dancing, showing off before the demure friend he had just made. And Herbert said his mother was seeking a live-in girl to help in her farmhouse kitchen, with some dairy work added. He suggested that she applied, but asked her not to say she knew him – he didn't want his father to think he had persuaded the girl to apply for the job.

Not understanding the motives behind this comment, Kitty decided she liked Herbert and so she sought out Mrs Longster from among the throng of farmers' wives.

Mrs Longster gave her a thorough testing. She asked Kitty about housework, about dairying, about milking and about cheese-making; there were questions about dress-making and sewing, patching and knitting, baking bread and making cakes ….

The result was that Kitty Garthwaite found herself employed at the Longster's big farm near Lowna, at the southern tip of Farndale. She was told she could live in, but as her own home was but a mile away, she could sleep at home if she wished, and if her duties permitted. Kitty was deliriously happy. How many girls found such a pleasant place to work so close to home? And there was Herbert … already, Kitty was dreaming of marriage.

Her mother had filled Kitty's pretty head with ideas of marrying the son of the wealthy Longsters and of one day becoming mistress of that household. She had said that the Longsters were not gentry, but yeomen farmers, no better than Kitty's dad, but fortunate in having had the farm handed down over the generations.

On 1 December, Kitty began her new job. For the first weeks, she lived in. The domestic quarters occupied one end of the Longsters' farmhouse and had their own staircase. There were three bedrooms each containing three small wooden beds; two of the rooms housed the male workers and one was used by the girls. All sparsely furnished, they offered little more than a bed and a cupboard, and the workers ate in the kitchen with the family and washed in the skullery.

Kitty's job was to help in the kitchen. She had to rise at half-past five to light the fire and cook breakfast for the family and all the workers. Breakfast was at seven, with ten o'clocks to prepare later, then dinner at twelve noon, tea at four and supper at half-past seven. It was during those meals that she would be in Herbert's presence. At first, he ignored her, albeit sometimes giving her a quick smile or a wink, but as she became more accustomed to the house and its routine, and as Herbert began to appreciate her beauty even more, he began to seek her out. When his mother was out seeing to the hens, and his father was at market in Kirkbymoorside, Herbert would look for Kitty and in no time, she fell madly in love with him.

He said he loved her too. He discovered that the saddle-room was often empty in the evenings, and that its continuously-burning peat fire kept it warm throughout the night. And so he began to take Kitty into that room with its smell of leather and saddle soap, its dusty warmth and its rows of horse blankets hanging from the beams as they aired in the dry heat. Even in winter, it was cosy.

And it was there, as Christmas approached, that Kitty first experienced the thrill of physical love, and it was two months later when Ralph Longster, Herbert's strict father, discovered what had been going on. It was now February with the nights getting lighter and the need for the workers to be available, but without listening for an explanation, he banished his son to a cousin's home at Pickering for a month and told Kitty she must go. He said other girls had been tempting Herbert with a view to becoming mistress of Dovecot Farm, but stressed he was not going to allow it. He wanted nothing immoral on his premises.

In tears, Kitty handed back the fastning penny, the coin

traditionally handed over by an employer at the beginning of the employment to bind the contract. With her meagre belongings in a hessian bag over her shoulder, Kitty trudged home.

With Herbert at an unknown address in Pickering, Kitty settled in at home, miserable, tearful and jobless. She received a little comfort from her mother but another more serious problem was looming. As March lengthened the days, Kitty was experiencing morning sickness and an entirely different feeling within herself ... she knew about animals and how they conceived ... she had worried about the risks when she'd been with Herbert, even though he'd said it would be all right. She was frightened now, and must ask her mother what was happening to her.

On Mothering Sunday that March in 1784, Kitty made her mother a simnel cake, the traditional gift on this day, and then, alone with her mother, she sought her advice. It took but a few minutes for Mrs Garthwaite to discover the truth.

Kitty was amazed her mother was not angry, but she was not; in fact, she was proud. Her Kitty ... running a spot like that ... marrying into yeomanry ... she'd have servants ....

Kitty waited until she felt Herbert must have returned from Pickering, then she walked across to the farm. She knew that every Saturday morning, Herbert took a cart over to Hutton-le-Hole where he did deals at the Hammer and Hand Inn before returning with perhaps a pig or a load of potatoes or even a barrel of beer. She waded across the ford at Lowna and settled to her wait near the gate to Dovecot Farm.

But when Kitty hailed Herbert and told him of her condition, he was very offhand with her. He refused to accept any responsibility, and said the father could be any of the stable lads. Then he whipped his horse into a trot and left her standing beside the road.

She shouted after him, but he never looked behind. She

ran alongside for a few yards, pleading with him and saying she'd not been with other boys, but his answer was to whip the horse into a clumsy gallop. She stood among the heather with tears streaming down her face as Herbert disappeared over the hill near Barmoor. In the days that followed, she tried several times to contact him, but he never allowed her to get near. She was totally isolated.

As she witnessed her daughter's deepening misery and increasing girth, her mother suggested that Kitty write a letter to Herbert, asking for a meeting. She felt that a face-to-face talk might convince Herbert that the child was his. With her mother's help, Kitty composed a short note asking Herbert to meet her just once, just one last time. And much to their surprise, a week later, a letter was pushed under the door of Kitty's cottage; it was from Herbert and it said, 'Meet me near Lowna Rock three next Saturday afternoon.'

Kitty was full of hope; Herbert's parents went to Kirkby-moorside on Saturday afternoons, so their meeting would be secret. Her mother told her to take a Bible and swear on it before Herbert that the child was his. Because his parents were staunch chapel folk, followers of John Wesley's new and strict teachings, that act should convince him of the truth. And so, on the morning of that April day, Kitty prepared for this vital meeting. But the storm clouds gathered; thunder crashed in the dale and torrential rain poured from the dense black clouds. In minutes, the dale tracks were awash with thick brown floodwater which poured from the hills. Cottages and farms were flooded, tracks were flowing like rivers and the carcases of drowned livestock like poultry and lambs were washed into the newly-formed streams and carried away. It was a cloud-burst of terrifying power and it swamped the little dale within minutes. Kitty stood at the door, praying that it would stop before she set out.

Her mother asked her not to brave the storm, but Kitty was determined and so she left the cottage. The rain was still pouring down, but the worst of the storm had passed.

With hessian sacks covering her head and shoulders, Kitty began the long walk to the Lowna Rock. The events which followed remain a mystery, although it is known that the ford at Lowna had been transformed into a raging torrent as water from the deluge had flowed into the narrow River Dove from its huge catchment area high in the dale and upon the surrounding moors. It was chest high at the ford, spilling several yards along the track and flowing swiftly downstream as it carried broken boughs, dead sheep and lambs, gorse bushes and tons of thick brown mud.

Standing in the track on the edge of the swirling water, Kitty watched it boil around her boots, but she could not see the boulder which was to be their meeting place; it was to the left of the track which climbed towards Hutton-le-Hole and to the right of Birch Hagg. Was Herbert waiting there? She knew that there was no other crossing place within miles. She *must* cross that river.

As she stood in her soaking clothes, a horseman was riding towards her, drenched like herself. He advised her not to go through as the flood had almost carried his horse away. Above the roar of the water, she asked if he had seen a lad at the other side, and he said he had passed someone riding into Kirkbymoorside, going through Hutton-le-Hole. Then he kicked his dripping horse into a gallop and head down against the storm, he rode from her sight.

We can only speculate about the thoughts going through poor Kitty's mind at that moment. Did she think Herbert had cruelly betrayed her; by riding away from her towards Hutton-le-Hole and then into Kirbymoorside, had he shown that he did not care for her at all? If it was Herbert, he should have been riding towards her, coming this way. Or was it another rider? Perhaps Kitty should attempt to wade that torrent? After all, the rider might have seen someone else, not Herbert; besides, that man had succeeded in crossing the flood, so if a horse could get through, then surely a strong girl could make it?

What we do know is that Kitty died in that river. Her naked body was found downstream from the ford and a few days afterwards, the drowned body of Herbert Longster was also found in the river.

The double tragedy stunned the dalesfolk and the story is still told today, albeit with various solutions to this mystery. One account says that Kitty, disillusioned by the thought that Herbert had finally rejected her, removed all her clothes, threw herself into the strong and fast-flowing water and drowned herself. Another theory is that her death was a pure accident; in attempting to wade across the flood to meet Herbert, she was swept to her death.

So how did Herbert meet his death?

One strong theory is that he had in fact decided to marry Kitty and in spite of floods and storms, had belatedly set off to Kirkbymoorside to buy a ring.

We cannot be sure of the timing of the horseman's sighting of 'a lad' in Hutton-le-Hole who was riding towards Kirkbymoorside. If this was Herbert, he had left it very late to buy a ring, setting out upon an eight-mile return trip about the time he'd arranged to meet Kitty. It presumed she would wait for a couple of hours or so. Furthermore, his route was the longer one from Lowna to Kirkbymoorside and perhaps this had been necessary because of the flooded ford. The normal route was via Gillamoor. Perhaps, in his late decision to marry Kitty, he'd decided to go immediately before the shops closed, and maybe he guessed she would not make the rendezvous due to the storm. Upon his return perhaps twc hours later, he may have tried to cross the swollen river, by then even deeper in flood, in order to ride to Kitty's home with his good news. But in struggling against the fierce flow, we can speculate that the horse threw him; he drowned in the very same water as his lover. The riderless horse survived and returned to Dovecot Farm; it was this which prompted the search which discovered both bodies next day.

So were these tragic deaths two accidents, two suicides or one suicide and one accident? The local people thought it was a double suicide; Kitty had killed herself because of Herbert's refusal to marry her, and Herbert had committed suicide because of the shame he had brought upon his strict and religious family.

For this reason, the couple were buried beside the road and not in a churchyard, this being the traditional treatment of suicide cases.

But could this be a case of murder and suicide? Or murder and accident? Perhaps Herbert, burdened by the thought that his immoral behaviour might become known to his parents, decided to end this danger by killing Kitty and making it appear to be an accident?

The possibility lies in the continuing legend attached to this sad story. When Kitty's body was found, she was naked and the story has become the legend of Sarkless Kitty. Sarkless is a local word; working girls often wore a rough dress known as a sark and when her body was discovered, Kitty was completely naked.

Let us assume that Herbert wanted to silence Kitty for ever because of the secret she held over him and his family. He would know that she would make strenuous efforts to arrive at the rendezvous point and that she would wait there for him, for a long time if necessary. By riding into Hutton-le-Hole, where he was well known, he established an alibi for the period around 7 p.m., the time he'd committed on paper for this meeting. Witnesses could state he was elsewhere at the time of Kitty's death. Besides, would he really ride into Kirkbymoorside to buy a ring when his parents were known to be there? Having ridden to Hutton-le-Hole, however, he could ride back in time to meet the waiting Kitty. She would be marooned by the flood.

He would then cross the raging ford on horseback, kill

Kitty, remove all her clothes to prevent identification of the body, and ride home. But, in attempting to return across the floodwaters, his horse must have shied, tossing him into the waters to perish in the very manner of his lover. Or, having killed her, did he then commit suicide during a fit of remorse? Or to avoid facing his own disgrace? Whatever happened, the riderless horse returned home and a search was mounted, the bodies being found the next day, a Sunday, after the awesome flood had subsided.

The possibilities are almost endless; the fact that Kitty's body was naked does suggest she was murdered, but it also suggests another theory which I have never seen published. This is my theory.

Let us suppose that the horseman's sighting of Herbert was correct, and that Kitty waited patiently and hopefully beside that raging stream for Herbert to visit her. He would be late, having ridden into town to buy a ring, but Kitty waited. Due to the flood, she could not wade across to their meeting place, and so Herbert, with the ring in his pocket, attempted to ride his horse towards Kitty. This meant passing through the dangerous, rushing waters. The horse shied or perhaps it was washed off its feet and it threw him off. He struggled and shouted, but the weight of his sodden riding gear dragged him under ... the horse galloped to safety but Kitty could only watch as her lover was swept helplessly downstream. He was drowning ....

What could she do?

In a supremely brave attempt to save his life, she stripped off her own clothing – her sark – to make her efforts in the water that much safer and then waded in to reach her drowning Herbert. But the current was too strong and she was swept away to her sad and untimely death.

This, I feel, is probably the real solution and it is supported by one account which says that when Herbert's body was recovered, there was a wedding ring in his pocket. I believe that Kitty did not die a suicide, nor was she murdered. The evidence, slight though it is, suggests that she died in a tremendous show of bravery as she fought to save her lover and their unborn child. She fought so hard to secure her future but lost everything.

The people of the time thought they had committed suicide; they were buried beside the road but an elderly Quaker from Farndale decided to give them a decent burial. At night and in great secrecy, he exhumed the remains and reburied them in the little Quaker burial-ground on the west banks of the River Dove at Lowna, not far from the scene of her death. Between 1675 and 1837, some 114 Quakers were buried there and the site is still marked by a plaque. That kindly man died in Farndale and is buried there, but his descendants live in the Middle West of the USA.

Kitty and her lover are now at peace but we shall never know the precise circumstances of their sad deaths.

Farndale's second mystery is far more brutal and grisly, and it involves a remote farmhouse at Middle Head, described as the topmost dwelling in the valley. This old thatched building, once known as Middlehovet, was last occupied in 1920 since when it has fallen into ruin. Running across the moors above the old farmstead was an ancient track which ran from Ingleby Bank Top, across the head of Farndale and then down the eastern side of the dale before branching over the moors towards the Lion Inn at Blakey. Favoured by packhorses and carriers, it was also used by people traversing that wild and bleak region on foot.

One autumn in the eighteenth century, there had been a pig-killing day on the remote farm and that same night, the farmer's wife, whose name we do not know, was busy making saim. This is a form of lard made after a pig-killing from the leaf (the layer of fat which enclosed the kidneys) and the rutting fat. Left alone during her husband's short absence, she was very busy and was prepared to work all night to boil down the fat.

As she worked, someone knocked on her door and she was surprised to see a large woman standing there. She had come down from the moorland track, having seen the lamps burning at the windows, and begged for a night's accommodation. The woman stressed she did not want a bed; she was happy to sleep on the floor for she sought only shelter and rest until the morning.

The farmer's wife, perhaps feeling that some female companionship during the long night hours would be very welcome, offered her the squab which was in the kitchen.

A squab was a crude kind of sofa; this one was made of oak and had a narrow wooden bed which could be laid upon it and so the visitor said this was perfect. She had something to eat and drink, and then watched as the farmer's wife continued her lard-making. Gradually, as the night wore on, the visitor's weariness overcame her and she seemed to fall asleep on the hard squab. The wife ignored her for a while, being content to let her guest slumber as she worked, but then, glancing down at the still form, she had a shock.

Peeping from underneath the outer garments was a huge pair of male boots. Careful inspection in the dim light suggested that only the outer garments were female; beneath was a huge man and he was not asleep. He was pretending, for now she could see the flickering of his eyelids.

Why wear such disguise if it was not to rob the house and kill her when she fell asleep? Why pretend to be asleep? There was no help nearby and so the unfortunate farmer's wife found herself in a serious dilemma. How could she prevent herself being attacked and the house from being robbed? The pan of hot pig fat, bubbling on her fire, provided the answer. She looked again at the man; his mouth was open and he was pretending to snore ...

In a trice, she lifted the pan of boiling fat from the fire and poured it down his throat. As the writhing man was dying his ghastly death, she dragged him outside and laid him on the midden, the local name for the dung-hill. Now terrified, she locked her doors and extinguished her lamps.

But she did not go to bed, for she felt sure the man would have an accomplice waiting outside for a signal to raid the house. Then, in the early hours of the morning, she heard someone whistle; this was the signal from the gang who were expecting their accomplice to unlock the doors.

'If it's your friend you seek!' she cried. 'You'll find him on the midden!'

Next morning, the body had disappeared. Had they buried it and if so, where? Just behind Middle Heads Farm was a belt of rock under which rabbits had burrowed, and the last tenant, before the house was deserted in the 1920s, was ferreting there. One of his ferrets entered the holes among the rocks but did not return; he scoured the area searching for it and found a roughly built dry-stone wall among the rocks. It formed a small shelter by using a slab of stone as a roof, and when he managed to peer inside, he found a human skull.

Was it the body from Middle Head Farm? Neither the wife nor the accomplices would bury it on the midden because when that was eventually used as manure, it would reveal the corpse. Neither wanted it linked to them, consequently this band of rocks, very close to the farm, provided a quick and ideal hiding-place where only wild animals would find it.

Was this murder or self-defence? No one was prosecuted and no one knows the identities of the parties involved. Maybe the story is nothing more than a moorland tale, but the discovery of that skull does suggest otherwise.

4   Coxwold's Famous Bodies

There seems little to link Oliver Cromwell, Puritan and Lord Protector of England, with the 'lascivious' author Laurence Sterne, one of the first humorous novelists.

In those hectic and dangerous political times which led to the abolition of both the Monarchy and the House of Lords, Oliver Cromwell (1599-1658) had overthrown the Crown, brought about the execution of Charles I and had then, in 1653, assumed power over the misnamed Free State as the oppressive Lord Protector of England.

Laurence Sterne (1713-1768), on the other hand, was born in Ireland some fifty-five years after Cromwell's death. He came to Yorkshire and, from the age of ten, received his education at Hipperholme School, near Halifax. He became a clergyman in the Church of England and later surprised both the church hierarchy and the public by writing popular and highly satirical novels, some of whose passages were considered obscene. He became rich and famous, and is now a major international figure because of his literary work.

In life, their paths never crossed; that would have been impossible, but after death there are striking parallels. The body of each man was exhumed and mutilated. Then, in circumstances of some mystery, each corpse was brought from London to the same tiny North Yorkshire village to be reburied. Now, in death, these two great men from widely differing spheres of English history, lie less than a mile apart.

Or do they?

The village in question is Coxwold, surely one of Yorkshire's most beautiful. Small, compact and highly attractive, it is replete with points of interest. Lying almost in the shadows of Sutton Bank, whose summit is known for its enthralling views across Yorkshire, Coxwold is the most southerly village of the North York Moors National Park. Nearby is Kilburn with its famous White Horse carved in the hillside above the workshops of Mousey Thompson. He was a village wood-carver whose tradition continues with the trademark of a mouse; a tiny mouse is carved on every piece of furniture, all of which is executed in mature oak at Kilburn and sold across the world. Rievaulx Abbey, Byland Abbey and Ampleforth Abbey are nearby too, along with some of North Yorkshire's most dramatic and interesting countryside. It contains fascinating market-towns, pretty villages, old abbeys, castles and imposing stately homes.

But Coxwold stands apart. In some ways, it is unique for within the length of one main street is a magnificent and historic Perpendicular church with an octagonal tower, an ancient manor house called Colville Hall, a charming inn called the Fauconberg Arms, an old grammar school dating from 1603, almshouses built during the reign of Charles II, and a modern pottery, plus some other shops from which purchases can be made. The long wide street is gently sloping with wide, neatly-trimmed grass verges and the pretty houses are built of local yellow limestone beneath red pantile roofs.

It presents a most charming picture and offers constant delight to residents and villagers alike. But there are additional places of great interest at Coxwold. At the top of the same street, just beyond the church where Sterne is said to be buried, is Shandy Hall. This intriguing old house, now occasionally open to the public, was once the home of Laurence Sterne and is now an internationally-known literary shrine in his honour. A short distance beyond the foot of the same street is the magnificent Newburgh Priory, which is also occasionally open to the public. Founded in 1145 as an Augustinian priory, it is now a superb and interesting house with wonderful gardens. It is believed that this house contains the remains of Oliver Cromwell.

So are both Oliver Cromwell and Laurence Sterne really buried at Coxwold?

Oliver Cromwell can be described as a religious and military fanatic; he used the Army to impose Puritanism upon this country after a hectic childhood. Stories tell us that he was once seized by an ape and carried to the roof of his parents' house. Later, he was rescued from drowning by a clergyman and once dreamt that he would become the greatest man in England. As a youth, he was always fighting, for he loved the physical effort of brawls, combat and even athletics. In his youth, he studied a curious combination of law, theology and military works, later turning to politics.

He was something of a hypochondriac, often thinking he was dying, but he had great drive and enthusiasm for his self-imposed tasks. When he inherited an estate in the Isle of Ely, he devoted himself to agriculture and prevented the draining of the fens, an act for which the grateful local people called him 'Lord of the Fens.'

In appearance, he was not very impressive. When he appeared in Parliament, it was said 'He was very ordinarily apparelled in a plain cloth suit made by a country tailor, his linen plain and not clean, his hat without a hat-band. His stature of a good size, his sword stuck close to his side, his countenance swollen and reddish, his voice sharp and untuneable and his eloquence full of fervour.' Another account says, 'He was abstemious, temperate, indefatigably industrious, and exact in his official duties. His exterior inspired neither love nor confidence; his figure had neither dignity nor grace, his conversation and manner rude and vulgar, his voice was harsh. On the other hand, he possessed extraordinary penetration and knowledge of human nature; no one knew so well the art of winning men and using them to his purpose.'

He was aware of his unbecoming appearance, for when he had his portrait painted, he told the artist, 'I desire you would use all your skill to paint my picture truly like me, and not flatter me at all. But remark all these roughnesses, pimples, warts, and everything as you see me, otherwise I will never pay a farthing for it.'

It was this instruction which has come down to us in the form of the saying 'warts and all', meaning a total picture of a subject, including blemishes.

But a career both with the army and in politics, each fired by a puritanical devotion to God, turned him into a national and international figure. He reached the peak of his career on 16 December 1653 when, with the King executed, he was sworn in as Lord Protector of England. This made him master of a powerful army and a strong fleet. With his Council, he had the authority to issue Ordinances which had the effect of law, and he was very concerned that there should be religious freedom of conscience, except to Catholics. It is unnecessary to go into a detailed account of his life, save to say that the five years between 1653 and 1658 were a very heavy burden, due to the problems he faced both at home and overseas. They taxed even his strong, if narrow-minded, faith in God and his powerful constitution. Even for a man who thrived on conflict, he endured much, particularly during his final years.

His five years as Lord Protector aged him rapidly; he was plagued by a constant barrage of supposed conspiracies and worried about attacks on his life. He never travelled without an armed guard and always wore a shirt of protective mail under his clothes. In his ailing years, as he worried increasingly about his health, he took medicines so powerful that they affected his sanity and he suffered from a fever which recurred every three days and drained his strength.

On 3 September 1658, at the height of his prestige, Oliver Cromwell died. His eldest surviving son, Richard, then almost thirty-two, succeded his father as Lord Protector but he lacked the power and drive of his father. He resigned the following May and in 1660 fled to live in secret on the continent under the name of John Clarke. It was in 1660 that the monarchy was restored and the thirty-year-old Charles II became King of England. On 29 May 1660, the new King entered his capital to a universal and almost fanatical welcome, albeit mindful of what Cromwell had done to the throne and to his family.

At Newburgh Priory in Coxwold, these historic events were followed with more than the usual degree of concern. Thomas, Lord Fauconberg, 2nd Viscount and 1st Earl had reason to observe the events very closely, but more especially because he was married to Oliver Cromwell's third daughter, Mary. They lived at New-burgh Priory. Mary Cromwell was Lord Fauconberg's second wife. His first had been Mildred Saunderson, daughter of Viscount Castleton, but she had died very young in 1656. In seems that Lord Fauconberg was a most ambitious man, with an acute sixth sense which enabled him to anticipate momentous events. He mixed with, and was related to, many powerful people who shaped the future of the nation. Upon the death of his first wife, therefore, he recognised the opportunites open to him by cultivating Oliver Cromwell, who was by then Lord Protector of England.

These efforts led to his marriage to Mary and so Lord Fauconberg became Cromwell's son-in-law. This mar-riage, which, like his first, produced no children, was in 1657, the year following the death of his first wife. One legend says that a condition of the marriage, imposed by Cromwell, was that all the oak trees in the grounds of

Newburgh Priory, should have their tops cut off. The union rapidly produced honours for Thomas. He was given a position in the new House of Peers and a year later was sent as Ambassador to the Court of Louis XIV of France. Cromwell certainly made use of him, although there is doubt about Thomas's total loyalty. Always ambitious and able to anticipate events, it seems that when Cromwell died, Thomas was already looking around for new openings. He realized that the monarchy was likely to be re-established and so he set about changing his loyalty by making useful contacts among the Royalists. Thus, it seems, he learned of the acts of revenge about to be perpetrated upon the dead Cromwell and his supporters.

In 1658, Cromwell had been buried in Westminster Abbey and in 1657, so had Admiral Robert Blake, Commander of Cromwell's navy, and the Puritan politician John Pym (1653). Other Cromwell supporters who had gone to their graves in Westminster Abbey included John Bradshaw (1659), a judge of the High Court of Justice and president of the court of dubious legality which had condemned Charles I to his death, and Henry Ireton, the general who led Cromwell's army. Ireton, like Lord Fauconberg, was Cromwell's son-in-law, having married Bridget Cromwell in 1646. He died of the plague in Ireland five years later.

The Royalists decided to take their revenge upon these bodies and in 1661, they exhumed the corpses. Those of Pym and Blake were cast onto the ground outside the abbey, being removed to the dust of St Margaret's graveyard where they were abandoned. The bodies of Oliver Cromwell, Judge Bradshaw and Henry Ireton were, by order of the King, taken to Tyburn where they were hanged upon the gibbets and left to suffer desecration by the onlookers. One account says that Cromwell's head was later cut off and his body buried beneath the gibbet.

But the craftiness and advance planning made by the cunning Lord Fauconberg paid dividends. His contacts among the Royalists enabled his wife to secure her father's body minus its head before further desecration was caused. It was not buried under that gibbet. Instead, Mary travelled to London with some trusty companions in conditions of the utmost secrecy and, through her husband's great influence, managed to obtain the corpse. It was brought to Newburgh Priory, where it was hidden in a tomb specially constructed high in the roof gables. No one would find it there. Later, the roof of the house was raised and so the tomb was revealed where it can now be seen by visitors in an upstairs room. A small plaque tells of the contents and a copy of Cromwell's death mask is on top of the brick-built tomb.

But does this pile of bricks really contain the headless body of the first Lord Protector of England? The answer is that no one knows because the tomb has never been opened. In spite of constant pressure to open it, the family has never allowed any examination of its contents and all attempts have failed. There is on record the story of King Edward VII (1841-1910). He was the eldest son of Queen Victoria and when he was Prince of Wales, he was a guest at Newburgh Priory. When the family were otherwise engaged, he persuaded the estate carpenter to break into the tomb, but the plotting pair were caught in the act and Cromwell's tomb remains intact, the contents even defying a royal wish to inspect them, and so the mystery remains.

A visit to Newburgh Priory will be rewarded with many reminders of Cromwell. A portrait of his daughter, Mary, the Countess of Fauconberg can be seen; a caption on the painting wrongly states that she was his second daughter, for she was his third. In the Black Gallery there is a portrait of Cromwell himself and throughout the house there are other items which once belonged to the Lord Protector, including a fine silver pen and a saddle.

There is no doubt that Newburgh Priory contains a wealth of Cromwellian influences, but does it also contain his body?

The case of Laurence Sterne's body has comic elements which could have provided a basis for one of his books. Sterne was a strange but likeable man who had endured a tough childhood. Born to poverty in Ireland in 1713, he experienced a hard time during which four of his six brothers and sisters died in infancy. In the first ten years of his life he travelled with his soldier-father and his mother, living in either barracks or inns. When he was ten, he came to Yorkshire where his uncle acted as his guardian, and he was educated at Hipperholme School near Halifax.

While he was there, his father died in Jamaica where his regiment was serving, and his mother was struggling to keep her surviving family together in Ireland. She had no time for Laurence and it was fortunate that his cousin, Richard Sterne who was the young Squire of Elvington Hall near York, took an interest in him and sent him to Cambridge University. At university, he made a firm friend of John Hall-Stevenson of Skelton Castle near Saltburn, and in later life spent many hilarious and happy hours there.

Upon graduation, Laurence Sterne joined the Church of England as a deacon; his patron was his uncle, Dr Jaques Sterne who was a Precentor of York Minster and also Archdeacon of Cleveland. Through his influence, Laurence was eventually offered a living as vicar of Sutton-on-the-Forest, a village near Easingwold in the North Riding of Yorkshire. He then became a canon of York Minster in 1741 at the age of only twenty-eight.

It was during his time at York that he met and married Elizabeth Lumley. She was daughter of the Vicar of Bedale and had been living in the Minster Yard at York, but she was not an easy woman to live with, nor was he the most amiable of husbands. One account of Mrs Sterne says 'She does the right things but in a very unpleasing manner'. The couple returned to Sutton where they tried to settle to village life, at one stage buying a farm only to make a mess of running it. In 1744, Sterne was appointed vicar of Stillington, the village next to Sutton. His daughter Lydia, to whom he became devoted, was born here in 1747, the only survivor of several children, and it was at Stillington in 1759, that he discovered his gift as a comic author.

He wrote a satirical work called *A Political Romance* which was later burnt because it upset the Archbishop, but he then settled down to write *The Life and Opinions of Tristram Shandy, Gentleman*. This was rejected by a publisher in London, and about the same time, both Sterne's mother and his uncle Jaques died and his wife suffered a mental breakdown. She was placed in the care of a specialist doctor and in a sad, lonely mood, he rewrote his book in novel form. He borrowed some money and had the first two thin volumes printed in York, then asked a London publisher to distribute copies in the city. In 1760, he was taken to London in a friend's coach and he went into the City to seek copies of his book. None was to be found. The book had sold out. It was a huge success.

He was then asked to write more volumes about Tristram Shandy, and to produce collections of his sermons. Quite suddenly, Laurence Sterne was both successful and famous as a novelist. There was surprise that the author of such bawdy tales was a clergyman, and it was during the fuss about his books, and during the warmth and esteem showered upon him by his admirers, that Lord Fauconberg offered him the living at Coxwold.

Sterne accepted with the utmost pleasure, for this was indeed a fine village. His wife's health had improved and so, with his wife and daughter Lydia, he moved to Coxwold. Here he could complete the remaining volumes of *Tristram Shandy*, and there is no doubt that he was blissfully happy in the house he rented at Coxwold. The unorthodox vicar filled the church with those who wanted to hear his sermons and caused them to chuckle when he said that those who liked him could face him in church, while those who didn't might face the other way. He walked the land around Coxwold, crossing the plains near Byland Abbey or climbing to the moors behind, sometimes rushing back home to jot down an idea or a line he had just created.

He called his house Shandy Hall, after the fictitious home of the Shandy family in his novel, and altered it to suit his odd tastes. Some of his bizarre ideas can still be seen. Although he spent a lot of time in London, it was to Shandy Hall that he returned to write. He liked the fresh air, the solitude and the surrounding countryside.

Here he completed his *Tristram Shandy* books, much to the concern of the bishops and the delight of his readers. But in spite of his fine life and success, Laurence Sterne was not a well person. Even as a young man, he had suffered haemorrhages of the lungs, a sure sign of tuberculosis, and now, at the height of his fame, there were indications that the disease was growing steadily worse. On a visit to London, he became very ill, but he was determined to survive and in fact went off to Paris. This was in January 1762. But he was ill there, at one stage lying speechless for three days. His wife and daughter joined him, but his wife decided to live there permanently.

Laurence came back to Coxwold to write, sometimes visiting York, Skelton Castle and London; in London, he fell in love with a twenty-three-year-old mother of two children whose husband was in Bombay, and who wished to become a writer; this was not the first of his love affairs, but it was not to survive. The young woman, Eliza Draper, returned to her husband, but their parting made Sterne fall ill. He returned to Coxwold, revived and in June 1767 wrote:

I am as happy as a prince at Coxwold and wish you could see how in princely manner I live. I sit down alone to venison, fish and wild fowl or a couple of fowls or ducks, with curds and strawberries and cream and all the plenty which a rich valley under the Hamildon Hills can produce; with a clean cloth on my table and a bottle of wine on my right hand, I drink your health.

He continued:

I have a hundred hens and chickens about my yard and not a parishioner catches a hare or rabbit or a trout, but he offers it to me. I am in high spirits; care never enters this cottage.

He managed to complete two of the intended four volumes of his *A Sentimental Journey through France and Italy* and wrote a daily 'Journal to Eliza', his departed love. He took the manuscript of *A Sentimental Journey* to London at Christmas 1767 where he enjoyed meeting his fans and friends. He remained in London until his book was published, but as it was being enjoyed by his readers, he fell gravely ill. He knew the end had come, and on 18 March 1768 he died aged fifty-four. His funeral was at St George's Church, Hanover Square, London, and he was buried in a new graveyard near Bayswater Road.

Then followed a strange sequence of events. Two days after his funeral, his grave was broken into by body-snatchers who sold the body for anatomical research. It was taken to Cambridge where a surgeon intended to use it during a lecture and demonstration on anatomy. The surgeon had even reached the stage of removing the top of the skull when someone recognized the corpse as that of the famous author, Laurence Sterne. This was confirmed and the lecture ended immediately, after which hurried instructions were given for the body to be quietly returned to its grave in London. And so it was.

There, the story might have ended and that churchyard might have been the final resting-place of Laurence Sterne, but another odd sequence of events followed.

At this stage, we can ask ourselves whether Sterne's body was really returned to the correct grave after being snatched because one peculiarity is that his original gravestone, which wrongly stated his date of death, never accurately marked his grave; the inscription said that the Reverend Laurence Sterne lay 'near to this place.' However, further problems arose during the First World War when the gravestones were moved so that the ground could be used for allotments, so making the precise location of Sterne's grave even more obscure.

And then, as recently as 1969, further complications arose. It was announced that the old graveyard was to be sold for redevelopment as flats. This news reached the Laurence Sterne Trust which owns Shandy Hall and which has filled it with Sterne's books and manuscripts, including the world's largest collection of first editions of his works. The Trust sought and obtained permission to exhume the body of Sterne. This time, he would be legally raised from his grave, for the Trust wished to transfer his remains to Coxwold for reburial in the village he loved.

The grave was therefore opened to reveal further complications because it contained five skulls and a number of bones. So which was Sterne?

Fortunately, one of the skulls was found to have its top sawn off, evidence of the earlier body-snatching story, and additional proof was provided when this skull was found to match the measurements of a bust of Sterne by the English sculptor Joseph Nollekens (1737-1823). Satisfied that these were indeed the remains of Laurence Sterne, the Laurence Sterne Trust had them taken to Coxwold where they were buried beside the south wall of St Michael's Church.

To complete this bizarre tale, Laurence Sterne now has two tombstones, both brought from London with his remains. The earlier one was erected *'by two brother Masons, for although he did not live to be a member of their Society, all his incomparable performances evidently proved him to have acted by Rule and Square.'* It goes on to say that Sterne was 'the man who, with gigantic stride, Mow'd down luxuriant folies far and wide' and that he was 'by fools insulted and by prudes accus'd' – this stone is white with black lettering and it stands against the south wall of Coxwold church. It begins 'Alas Poor Yorick' which is a reference to a character in *Tristram Shandy*, and then says 'Near to this place lyes the body of The Reverend Laurence Sterne, AM [sic], dyed September 13th 1768, aged 55 years.' It was full of errors, for he was in fact not quite fifty-five and he died on 18th March 1768, this date being corrected by the second stone which lies on the ground in front of the white one.

This calls him The Reverend Laurence Sterne MA and refers to him as '*The celebrated author of Tristram Shandy and The Sentimental Journey*', adding that his works were unsurpassed in the English language for richness and humour. In an account of this kind, there is little space for a selection of Sterne's wit and humour, but the following story is a worthy example. He became involved in a dispute with Dr John Burton in the Minster Yard at York, and Burton said, 'I never give way to a fool!' Sterne's immediate reply was, 'But I always do,' and he stepped aside.

I'm sure Sterne would have enjoyed the continuing grotesque humour which has followed his death, and also the mysteries which now surround his grave and that of Oliver Cromwell. By standing beside Sterne's grave, one can look across the lush valley to Newburgh Priory where Cromwell is buried and one can almost imagine Sterne's bawdy ghost standing there and waving at the puritanical spectre of Oliver Cromwell.

But are Sterne and Cromwell really buried at Coxwold? It is a question which will long continue to provoke discussion.

5   The Martyr of Egton Bridge

Nicholas Postgate, who was born at Egton Bridge around 1597, grew up to become the mildest of men and yet he died a most vicious death at York's infamous Knavesmire. He was then an old man of eighty-two and is remembered with love and pride more than three centuries later. He was born at the height of the persecution of Roman Catholics in England. Elizabeth I was Queen and among the punishments she had devised for priests was hanging accompanied by disembowelling and quartering with a range of tough penalties for lay people who persisted in adhering to this ancient faith.

In spite of the risks, Nicholas became a priest and he was not executed for murder, highway robbery or burglary; his crime consisted only of being a Catholic priest, evidence of which was obtained when he was caught baptizing a child. He died a cruel death to become the Martyr of the Moors, but his death resulted in two continuing mysteries. It was also just one dreadful outcome of the fake Popish Plot which had been sadistically concocted by Titus Oates.

In many ways, Postgate's life followed the pattern of Christ's; each was born in a humble situation and in each case, little is known of their formative years. In later life, each became a missionary who travelled peacefully while teaching the word of God, then each was betrayed for money and for political reasons. Finally, each died an agonizing death but forgave those whose actions led to their executions. And each is still remembered.

In spite of his fame, very little is known of Nicholas Postgate's early life. It is known, however, that he came from a family whose members had suffered heavy fines for adhering to their faith and although certain references have come to light about his younger days, there is little to verify them. It seems that he was the youngest of the three sons of James and Margaret Postgate, his brothers being Matthew and William. His father was a farmer or farm worker and he was born at Kirkdale House, a humble cottage beside the River Esk at Egton Bridge deep in the North York Moors.

Egton Bridge lies in the Esk Valley, some eight miles from Whitby. A tiny community, it is known for its massive Catholic Church of St Hedda and its annual show of giant gooseberries held on the first Tuesday of August. The church contains relics of Father Postgate's ministry and even the local pub is called the Postgate. Kirkdale House, the birthplace of Father Postgate, is thought to have stood immediately on the left when travelling towards Goathland as one crosses the iron bridge which spans the Esk at Egton Bridge. The remains are said to have been visible within living memory, with children of St Hedda's RC Primary School playing in the ruins. I was a pupil at St Hedda's, but cannot recollect any sign of that old cottage in the 1940s. Maybe the awful floods of 1930 swept away the last remains, although the foundations may still be there. Today, regular pilgrimages are made to the site when thousands gather to hear an open-air Mass in the adjoining field.

On 5 July 1987, Cardinal Hume, the Cardinal Archbishop of Westminster and leader of Britain's Roman Catholics, celebrated Mass here to herald the beatification in Rome of Nicholas Postgate. In November 1987, eighty-five Roman Catholic martyrs, executed during the sixteenth and seventeenth centuries, were declared Blessed by the Pope in Rome, beatification being one step from canonization as a saint. Nicholas Postgate was one of that number.

Among the stories of the childhood of Nicholas Postgate is one which suggests that, in January 1616, he was fined ten shillings at Helmsley Quarter Sessions for being a member of a band of wandering players who were found begging. They were performing music and plays which were critical of the Protestant religion and the authorities tried to prevent them. This Nicholas Postgate was then described as a thirteen-year-old farm labourer from Egton. We do not know whether this was the same Nicholas, for our Nicholas would probably have been a few years older, assuming his date of birth is reasonably accurate.

What is beyond doubt, however, is that on 4 July 1621, our Nicholas Postgate became a student at the English College at Douai in France. He was there to become a Catholic priest, a vocation which was illegal in England. For that reason, potential Catholic priests had to be trained overseas and often assumed false names to avoid penalties being imposed upon their families in England.

The College had trained many priests and martyrs, several of whom had been executed long before the birth of Nicholas Postgate. At College, Nicholas Postgate called himself Whitmore or Whitemore, perhaps a witty reference to the fact that his home was in Blackamoor, as the area of the North York Moors around Egton Bridge was then known. He was later to use the names of other Catholic families, some of whom continue to live in that area, in particular the Watsons to whom he was related. Postgate was rather older than the average student, but he worked hard and took an active part in the running of the College. On 23 October 1627, there is a note to say he was the sacristan, during which he gave good service. He was ordained on 20 March 1628. He was now Father Postgate, the name by which he is still known in and around Egton Bridge. When I was a small child at Egton Bridge school, I thought he was still alive, so vivid were the accounts of his work and so much was he discussed and honoured in the area; at school, we even sang a hymn he had written while in prison at York and the activities of Father Postgate were discussed as if he had immediately preceded the priest then in charge of that historic parish.

On 29 June 1630, Father Nicholas Postgate returned to England. His job was to join the English Mission, in other words to revive the Catholic faith which had suffered so much during the Reformation and at the hands of the Protestant persecutors.

Many martyrs had been executed, many of whom came from the north-east, but this only strengthened Postgate's resolve to fight for his beliefs. It is possible that he landed at Whitby; there were strong links between the North Riding of Yorkshire and the College of Douai, and many priests, returning secretly to England, had landed at Whitby. The Abbey could not shelter them for it had been dissolved in 1539; nor could the little chapels and churches on the moors, they had been taken from the Catholics and placed in Protestant hands. This meant that the incoming priests had to rely for their shelter upon several large houses in the Whitby area.

These were 'safe houses' or 'clearing houses' where the incoming priests were allowed to sleep and eat until they could travel in safety to their new livings. Lady Catherine Scrope, widow of Lord Scrope of Bolton kept the Abbey House at Whitby and sheltered priests. Bagdale Old Hall at Whitby and Ugthorpe Hall (which had priests' hiding-places) were others, along with Grosmont Priory, Bridge-holme Green at Egton Bridge, Upsall Castle near Thirsk and a house in the Shambles at York. This was organized by Margaret Clitherow, now St Margaret Clitherow; her home is now a place of pilgrimage. The doors of these houses were left open, with food and drink always on the table, so that incoming priests could arrive and depart unseen. Bridge-holme Green at Egton Bridge had seven doors, a wonderful asset for enabling priests to dodge the pursuivants.

Clearly, a massive and highly efficient undercover organization was at work to aid the priests and Father Postgate was one of its benefactors. Like many secretive priests of his time, he became chaplain to a family who occupied a large country-house, in his case, to Lady Hungate at Saxton Hall near Tadcaster. For the next thirty years, he worked as chaplain to families resident at several manor-houses in the North, East and West Ridings of Yorkshire. He was also priest to the people who lived and worked on the estate and nearby. To disguise his genuine role, he operated and dressed as a gardener, a skill at which he was proficient and which he enjoyed.

Many of the locations remain – Hazlewood Castle near Tadcaster is now a retreat house and conference centre; in Postgate's days, it was the seat of the Vavasours, a most distinguished Catholic family. Nicholas Postgate also served at Burton Constable in East Yorkshire as chaplain to 'the old lady Dunbar'; at Everingham with a junior branch of this family; at Kilvington Castle near Thirsk with the Meynells and at other places throughout Yorkshire. For a priest, chaplaincy to the landed gentry did provide some safety and security, even if priests were treated more like servants than priests. It is something of a mystery, therefore, as to why Father Postgate gave up his life of reasonable comfort and security in exchange for the tough and lonely life of a missionary priest on the wild and inhospitable North York Moors.

This work, in addition to the discomforts of rough living, was also fraught with danger from the Protestant authorities. In spite of the risks and the physical hardship, Father Postgate, who was over sixty years of age, returned to his beloved moors to live and to work among the poor. Perhaps he had always identified with the moorland folk, especially the poor? Perhaps, in the belief that he was coming to the end of his life, he wished to spend his final days with the people he knew and loved? But he was not to know that he had a further twenty years or so of very tough and even exciting missionary work ahead of him.

Whatever the reasons for his return to Eskdale, he decided that his future work for God would be in and around the area of his birth. During the early months of 1660, he arrived at Ugthorpe. This small village stands on the moors above Egton Bridge, and is about six miles inland from Whitby with expansive views across the heather and towards the North Sea. He settled in a tiny, remote cottage just over two miles from Egton Bridge and about a mile from Ugthorpe; today, the site of that cottage is called the Hermitage, and parts of its walls are built into the farm buildings which stand upon its foundations.

In Postgate's time, the thatched cottage was described as lowly and of the poorest imaginable, being more like a cattle shed than a house. Only a single chimney identified it as a dwelling.

There was one low door through which visitors had to stoop to enter, and inside were two small rooms. With rough stone floors, the smaller was a bedroom containing a raised portion which housed the simple bed, and in the other room there was a fireplace to burn peat. Around the cottage, Father Postgate cultivated the moorland and planted flowers; even on this remote spot, his love of gardening surfaced and he grew daffodils which he knew as Lenten Lilies. These flourished long after his death, but were picked by pilgrims with misplaced ideas of perpetuating their loyalty – the flowers vanished.

From this lonely spot, Father Postgate decided to concentrate upon his flock of Catholics in and around Egton, Grosmont, Glaisdale, Ugthorpe, Sleights and Whitby, but inevitably, his travelling extended much further. He went over the moors to Guisborough in the north-east, and to the Pickering and Helmsley areas in the southern part of the North Riding. Many of those places are recorded in his life story, although he travelled in disguise as a pedlar or a jobbing gardener. His life was always at risk and there was constant danger from local informers and pursuivants.

In these desolate surroundings, therefore, Father Postgate began his famous moorland ministry. In all weathers, and in the teeth of fearsome storms and snows, he tramped across the moors for the next twenty years, saying Mass in secret, baptizing, marrying and burying his flock and administering the sacraments of the banned church.

He was a familiar figure in his rough brown habit, rather like that of a monk. Over it in wet weather, he wore a white button-up cape of a canvas material and he usually carried a long staff to aid his walking. He hiked tremendous distances during his moorland ministry, for he could not afford a horse. He was generally thought to be a small wiry man whose rugged life had removed any excess weight from his body; he was fit too, although he suffered from a recurring throat infection. For this reason, he grew a beard which acted as a protection of his throat against the severe weather of those moors. White hair and blue eyes set in a rather bland pale face completed his picture and it is said he was deep thinking and highly intelligent, with an interest in music and literature as well as gardening. He was very proper in everything he did and could be described as serious-minded, although he did possess a gentle sense of humour and an unconquerable cheerfulness.

As a travelling priest, he would carry certain items for use during Mass, such as a collapsible chalice, a small box with a secret locking system or cloth pyx for carrying the Sacred Host, small candles and altar condiments, missal, rosary and even a tiny altar stone made of slate. The items he carried would be small enough to be concealed and not readily identified as the artefacts of a Catholic priest. Equipped in this way, Father Postgate trekked around the moors as he undertook his self-imposed mission with enormous fervour and fortitude.

He conducted Mass in the barns, lofts and quiet rooms of farmhouses and cottages, many of which remain today.

One of them is the Mass House at Egton. It is situated on the right of Egton Bank, halfway between Egton Bridge and Egton as one climbs the hill. This sturdy stone-built cottage bears the legend 'Mass House' carved in stone on its south-facing wall. Postgate made use of it as a chapel and issued notice of forthcoming services through a code which involved spreading white sheets on the hedgerows. As this was the method used by the country folk for drying their washing, it was the perfect method of secret communication.

Another secret sign comprised five vertical lines etched into the stone above the doorways of houses and cottages. Said to represent the five wounds of Christ, this sign was an indication that travelling priests were welcome inside, and that there was also a rear door through which a swift exit could be made in case of a sudden raid by pursuivants. Indeed, the Mass House at Egton had a secret exit which led from the roof into the grounds outside, and there are tales of Father Postgate making several flights by this route to gain freedom in the woods which then surrounded the cottage.

In 1830, this house provided a surprise for the local people. A girl was cleaning the upper wall of the kitchen when the plaster gave way; she had uncovered a small, dark loft 15 feet long by 10 feet wide and 5½ feet high. A tunnel through the thatch provided a view of the outside and some of the congregation stood in the kitchen to hear Mass.

When the chapel was examined, it revealed an altar laid out for the celebration of Mass. There was a crucifix, a pair of candlesticks, a missal and even the priest's vestments. After more than 150 years, one of Father Postgate's secret loft chapels had been discovered and those relics, with many more, can be seen in St Hedda's Church at Egton Bridge. Another surprise occurred in 1928 when the roof was being repaired. Twenty florins and six shillings from the reigns of Elizabeth I, Charles I and Charles II were discovered in the thatch, probably being a secret cache of money set aside for Father Postgate's use. These coins were placed on display in St Hedda's Church, but, most unfortunately, were stolen in the mid-1970s.

In his quiet and secretive manner, Father Postgate continued his work as a priest. It seems he made friends with Protestants and Catholics alike; his pleasant and friendly manner, and his wholehearted devotion to God and his church, endeared him to all. There seemed no reason why he should not continue this work without severe hindrance, for the authorities were growing more relaxed in their attitudes towards Catholic priests. Unofficially, they were allowed to practise their faith.

But far away in London, events were about to take a sudden, dramatic and horrific turn for the worse. There were to be many tortures and executions of Catholic priests, and one direct casualty was to be Father Nicholas Postgate, then aged 81.

London is some 250 miles away from Egton Bridge but the effect of rumoured plots was to reach this remote district. There was always talk of plots in the capital, with the Catholics being blamed for a whole series of troubles, including the Fire of London. There were some who hated Catholics and who were prepared to go to any lengths to secure their own futures by revealing plots which were supposedly being engineered by Catholics. Two such men were a pair of Protestant churchmen, the Revd Titus Oates aged twenty-eight, and the Revd Ezrael Tonge aged fifty-five.

Oates was a despicable character; ugly in appearance and grossly immoral in character, he was unreliable, a liar, a fraud, a womanizer and a perjurer. He had been ordained in the Protestant faith but became a Catholic and then returned to being a Protestant, all to suit the needs of the moment. He was, at one stage, the Protestant chaplain for the household of the Catholic Duke of Norfolk. In many of his posts, including a living in Kent and a naval chaplaincy, he was expelled for gross immorality.

Tonge, on the other hand, was a very articulate, highly imaginative and very clever man. He was a Doctor of Divinity, a scientist and teacher. He invented a system for teaching children to write and submitted a paper to the Royal Society on the movement of sap in plants. One of his written works was a critical book entitled *Jesuit Morals*.

But these two men had one thing in common; they bitterly detested Catholics.

Anxious to stir up trouble for Catholics, Oates claimed that on a trip to Madrid, he had discovered a plot being hatched by the Jesuits. He claimed they were plotting to kill Charles II to replace him with his brother James, Duke of York. James would thereafter rule under the direction of the Jesuits. He also claimed he had told the Jesuits he would return to England to kill Tonge for having written a book so critical as *Jesuit Morals*. He claimed the Jesuits were pleased with this idea, and gave him £50 for his expenses. In England, Oates and Tonge got together to expand this story, with Tonge's brains adding substance to the wild ideas presented by Oates. They produced forty-three charges, saying *inter alia* that the plot was to be enforced by the Jesuits at the instigation of Pope Innocent XI, that the Royal Physician, Sir George Wakeman, had been bribed to murder the King, that four Irishmen had been bribed to murder the King by stabbing him, and that two Jesuit priests were to shoot him. A massacre of Protestants would follow, with an invasion of Ireland from France.

Tonge's literary ability and imagination helped to fuel this plot and they claimed these plans had been approved by the Jesuits at the White Horse Tavern in the Strand, London on 24 April 1678. By devious means, they passed news of the plot to Charles II, but the King soon saw that the documents were forgeries and that the plot was ficti-tious. He also proved Oates was lying on important details and totally rejected the supposed plot as pure fiction.

But the pair of evil conspirators persisted and spread

news of the plot to a gullible public by word of mouth and rumour. Even so, and in spite of a general suspicion of Catholics, the supposed plot did not have the impact they desired and so, with intent to spread their rumours more widely and effectively, they decided to approach a magistrate. They selected Sir Edmund Berry Godfrey, a highly respected Protestant Justice of the Peace at Westminster in London. Among his friends were many Catholics, even though he was a staunch supporter of the Anglican Church, but there was a little mystery around Sir Edmund. He counted many criminals among his friends too, and there were questions about his methods of acquiring wealth. Maybe this man would listen to their plot? Maybe this evil pair had means of blackmailing Sir Edmund into listening to their fake plot and even into taking action?

He did listen. He took sworn statements from them and on 28 September 1678 accepted a package of papers from Tonge in which the charges had risen from forty-three to eighty-one. The conspirators now felt they were achieving some success.

On Saturday 12 October 1678, Sir Edmund left his home near the Strand and was last seen alive making his way up St Martin's Lane. He asked his way to Primrose Hill and was seen in Marylebone, all before 1 p.m. He was not seen again for five days. At around 6 p.m. on Thursday 17 October, a farmer and a baker were passing waste ground near Primrose Hill when they found the body of Sir Edmund.

He was fully clothed and lying face down with his sword transfixing the body to the ground. There was a superficial wound on his left shoulder while a vivid line around his throat suggested strangulation. His wallet remained, but his money had been stolen; his cravat and bands were missing, but his periwig and hat were on a bush close to the body; his glove lay on a hedge. Two boys who had been seeking a lost calf testified that the body had not been there on the Monday or Tuesday preceeding and the inquest recorded a verdict of murder. A £500 reward was authorized for the arrest of the killer(s).

Three Catholics called Green, Berry and Hill were arrested on very dubious evidence and on 21 February 1679 were executed for this crime. The general belief is that they were innocent, but the rumour spread that the killing was the work of Catholics because Sir Edmund was a very zealous Protestant. For Tonge and Oates, this was a wonderful opportunity to 'prove' the mischief being planned against the State by Catholics, and they made capital out of this murder. Their plot received a huge boost from this death. Fear of Catholics swept through the land, fanned into terror by Oates and Tonge, and so every Catholic was once again put at risk of fines, arrest and execution.

One man who decided to punish the Catholics for this killing was called John Reeves. He believed that there were more plots and became fanatically determined to detect them; in addition, he wanted to avenge the death of Sir Edmund.

John Reeves was the man-servant of the murdered Sir Edmund Berry Godfrey and an account says, 'He was an implacable enemy of Catholicks as the supposed murtherers of his Master.' Following the death of his master, and for reasons which we do not know, John Reeves travelled from London to Whitby in the North Riding of Yorkshire where he obtained employment as an exciseman. His work included the collection of excise duties and taxes and the gauging of the contests of casks, barrels and other containers. His work put him in close contact with other Government and local officials, an ideal position from which to learn of illegal activities, and to act upon the information he acquired.

During his duties, he came across Matthew Lyth who farmed at Red Barns Farm between Littlebeck and Ugglebarnby near Sleights and took an instant dislike to him. He learned that at a wedding Lyth had said, 'You talk of Papists and Protestants; but when the roast is ready, I know who shall have the first cut.' On another occasion at the home of William Cockerill, Lyth had said, 'A sorrowful Christmas, a bloody Fastness [Shrove Tuesday] and a joyful Easter.' Reeves interpreted these quotes as subversive talk and decided that Lyth was a suspicious person. He kept watch on Lyth's activities and learnt that Lyth's baby son was to be baptized. The officiating priest was to be none other than a Catholic by the name of Nicholas Postgate. The date of the baptism was set for Sunday 8 December 1678, accompanied by Holy Mass.

With rewards now being offered for the arrest of Catholic priests, Reeves could barely contain his happiness; he would avenge the death of Sir Edmund Berry Godfrey and would earn a little cash too. In the chill of that December day, he and his colleagues secretly watched the farm as the guests arrived for the baptismal service, noting the arrival of the small, aged priest in his familiar brown habit. And then, as Father Postgate was conducting the baptism, Reeves, along with William Cockerill who was the constable for Eskdaleside and Henry Cockerill, a mariner from Whitby, raided the farm. They claimed they were searching for arms and ammunition for use in furthering the Oates Plot. Matthew Lyth tried to prevent the search, but failed.

But instead of finding arms, Reeves testified later that he found 'a supposed Popish priest there called Postgate, and also Popish books, relics, wafers and several other things, all of which the said Postgate owned to be his. The said Postgate said he was called Watson but afterwards being called the name of Postgate, he owned that to be his right name.'

And so Father Postgate was arrested, along with two farmers who were friends and perhaps relations of Matthew Lyth; they were called Readman and Roe. Those family names still survive in the area and their members still follow the Catholic faith. Father Postgate was then taken before a magistrate where depositions were sworn by Reeves and the two Cockerills, plus a man called Robert Langdaile.

The magistrate was Sir William Cayley who lived at Brompton near Scarborough, some twenty miles away. Sir William was a member of the famous Cayley family and in taking the depositions, he was aided by his son, also called William. Father Postgate made a statement too, and endorsed some alterations to its wording by initialling the margin with 'N.P.' in a large, strong letters in his own handwriting. Sir William felt that there was sufficient evidence to present before a Judge and therefore committed Father Postgate for trial at York Assizes. He was taken to York where he was imprisoned in York Castle to await the hearing. It seems that more evidence was called for because in March, other witnesses were called to Brompton to make statements; they included Elizabeth Baxter, Elizabeth Wood and Richard Morrice, all of whom testified that Father Postgate had conducted Catholic services in their presence.

Father Postgate was in prison for about four months before his trial which took place at the guildhall in March during the Lent Assizes. He was not charged with any involvement in the Oates Plot, but with being a Catholic priest, contrary to *27 Eliz.1.2*, an Act passed almost a century earlier in 1585. It outlawed 'Jesuits, seminary priests and such like disobedient persons.' Contemporary accounts show that the judge did his best to have the prisoner acquitted, saying there was no proof of ordination, but the evidence of Elizabeth Wood, Elizabeth Baxter and Richard Morrice overruled any of the jury's reservations.

They felt there was ample evidence that Father Postgate was a Roman Catholic priest, and he was found guilty then sentenced to death. During his trial, he retained his calm appearance, losing his composure only once when

Elizabeth Baxter testified against him. She was a spinster aged about thirty. She had become an Anglican and said that when she was a Catholic eight or nine years ago, Father Postgate had offered Mass at Biggin House, Ugthorpe, the home of John Hodgson and very close to the Hermitage. He had administered Holy Communion and it is said that her testimony reduced him to tears. After his conviction, she came to his cell full of remorse and seeking his forgiveness. This he readily gave; he even gave her money to pay her way home.

He was then placed in a cell at York Castle to await his execution. He remained there for four months, during which he composed the famous hymn which is still sung at Egton Bridge during funerals and at other occasions. It begins

O Gracious God, O Saviour Sweet
O Jesus think of me,
And suffer me to kiss thy feet
Though late I come to thee.

Seven more verses followed, and the singing of these words continues to provide a direct link between Father Postgate. and today's parishioners who practise the faith on his old 'patch!' In November 1987, that hymn was sung at his beatification in Rome.

Matthew Lyth was kept in prison until after the priest's execution, but it seems Readman and Roe managed to secure their release by saying the harvest had to be gathered in, although there is a hint that they later testified against Father Postgate and agreed to relinquish their faith. The Readmans, Roes and Lyths remain staunch Catholics to this day, however. During his imprisonment, Father Postgate had many visitors, a privilege granted him by the sympathetic judge. Many were from the families he had served years earlier as a chaplain and for a time, it seemed that he might avoid execution. Many priests had been found guilty and simply kept in prison because the authorities were somewhat concerned about the effect of wholesale executions for what seemed a very trivial crime. But on 11 July 1679, the Privy Council issued an order about 'diverse Popish priests who have been condemned in several counties.' The instruction said that it was 'this day ordered by Their Lordships in Council that the respective judges who go the circuits where the said priests remain do forthwith give direction that they be executed according to law.'

Thursday 7 August 1679 was the date of Father Postgate's execution. Early that morning, two ladies called to see him, one being Mrs Fairfax, the wife of Charles Fairfax of York and the other a Mrs Meynell of Kilvington, near Thirsk. Both belonged to aristocratic families and for them, it was a time of great distress but they found the little priest very calm and in good spirits.

He wore new clothes brought by friends, for it was a tradition that martyrs wore new clothes as they went to meet their Maker; he also wore around his neck, a small bone crucifix bearing a simple carving; that crucifix is now preserved at Ampleforth Abbey.

Having said his farewells at York Castle, the frail old priest was placed on a sledge and hauled along Castlegate, over the Ouse Bridge and up the rough cobbled street of Micklegate. From there, he was taken to the Knavesmire, now the site of York Racecourse. It was then known as Tyburn and the place of execution is marked by a simple stone placed there in 1970. Sorrowful Catholics and Protestants lined the route and then, as he awaited the awful moment, Father Postgate gave his final address.

He told the assembled witnesses that he was dying for the Catholic faith, and not for the Plot. He asked the Sheriff to assure the King that he had never, at any time, wronged His Majesty and prayed that God gave the King grace and the light of truth. He forgave all who had in any way done wrong to himself and brought him to this death, and he asked forgiveness for them all. He was then taken away by the executioner. He suffered hanging, drawing and quartering, the penalty for priests. A contemporary account says, 'You saw him strangled by the hands of the Comon [*sic*] Hangman, you saw his head severed from his body, his brest [*sic*] opened and his heart cut out, and the little blood remained in his aged trunk you saw it spilt upon the ground.'

The top joint of the forefinger of each hand was cut off, since this is where he held the Sacred Host during Mass, then his friends, Catholic and Protestant alike, were given the body. It was taken away on a wheeled sled. Some of his clothes were sold to collectors and in the gruesome manner of the time, relics such as his hands, strands of hair, scraps of clothing stained with his blood, the hangman's rope, and other items were salvaged and kept as souvenirs. Many of these can still be seen in places like the Bar Convent Museum at York, Ampleforth Abbey, St Mary's College, Oscott, St Cuthbert's at Old Elvet in Durham, the Postgate Centre at St Hedda's Church, Egton Bridge and at other places. His chalice is still used at Mass, sometimes said close to the cottage where he born, and sometimes at Red Barns Farm where he was arrested.

And what became of John Reeves, the man who arrested him? Afterwards, Reeves suffered immense distress; he had received £3 for informing on Postgate, with a further £20 promised but never paid. Apparently, Reeves could not live with his conscience and committed suicide; he drowned himself in a deep pool at Bog Hole near Littlebeck. Ever since, that pool has been known as the Devil's Dump, and legend says no fish has since been caught there.

But with the death of this martyr, who was the last but one to die for his faith in this way, there remain two mysteries.

The first is – who really killed Sir Edmund Berry Godfrey and why? The men hanged for the crime were apparently chosen at random, and were convicted upon evidence secured from a witness by torture. The Lord Chief Justice of the time, Sir William Scroggs, was corrupt and the pressure he exerted resulted in their executions. History is adamant they were innocent and suggests that members of the Peyton Gang, a group of extreme Protestants and republican Whigs, may have been responsible. Or did Oates commit the murder and blame the Catholics as a means of adding fuel to his Popish Plot? It seems that shortly before his death, Godfrey had openly said he did not believe Oates, so perhaps he was silenced in this way? We may never know.

The second mystery is – where is Father Postgate buried? His torn body was taken away for burial by friends both Catholic and Protestant. A copper plaque was placed in the coffin and it bore these slightly inaccurate words,

Here lyeth that Rd and pious Divine Dr Nicholas Postgate who was educated in the English College at Doway. And after he had labour'd fifty years (to the admirable benefit and conversion of hundrd (sic) of souls), was at last advanced to a glorious crown of martyrdom at the city of York on the seventh of August 1679, having been a priest 51 years, aged 81.

Neither that plaque nor Father Postgate's body has been found.

6   Witches of Moor and Dale

No book of crime and mystery from the North York Moors would be complete without a note of the witches who operated here and an account of some of their activities. Even into this century, powerful stories circulated around the more remote dales and moorland communities, while evidence of their presence and influence can still be seen – if you know what to seek and where to look.

These stories do present something of a mystery because of the manner in which witchcraft tales have survived, although the behaviour of these women was once regarded as a crime with death as the penalty. The Witchcraft Act of 1563 prescribed death by hanging for anyone practising witchcraft with intent to kill or destroy, with a year's imprisonment for hurting people or destroying goods. Six hours in the stocks was a lesser penalty, with many poor old women being prosecuted. In the forty-five years of Elizabeth I's reign, there were more prosecutions for witchcraft than during the whole of the seventeenth century. The Witchcraft Act of 1604 continued to prescribe the penalty for witchcraft as death by hanging and the moorland witches were fortunate in operating at a distance from the evil witch-hunter, Matthew Hopkins. In one year between 1645 and 1646, he sent to the gallows more witches than all the other witch-hunters in England. The number of his victims is not known but is said to reach several hundreds. His first was Elizabeth Clarke, a poor, one-legged old woman who was tortured to make her confess.

It seems there were far fewer witch prosecutions in Yorkshire than any other county. Yorkshire commonsense appeared to prevail and an example occurred at Thirsk in 1611 when Elizabeth Cooke appeared at the Quarter Sessions charged with cursing her neighbours and their belongings. The judge could not accept this as a serious charge and he dismissed the case, saying that all neighbours cursed one another from time to time. In 1623, a witch was freed at Doncaster after the judge refused to believe she could kill from a distance. Among the few executions were Mary Pannel who was hanged at Ledston in 1603 and Old Wife Green who was burnt in the Market Square at Pocklington in 1631. Petronal Haxley, a smith's wife, was also executed at Pocklington as a witch. Isabella Billington, aged thirty-two, was burnt at York on 5 January 1648; she had crucified her mother at Pocklington, following which she had sacrificed a cock and calf to Satan.

Although many witches were burnt, burning was not the legal penalty for witchcraft in England. All other European countries, including Scotland, executed their witches by burning. In England, however, when witches were burnt to death, the crime with which they were charged would probably have been murder, treason or heresy, not witchcraft. Isabella Billington is an example of this; she was burnt as a murderess, the witchcraft elements being secondary to the crime, but she has since been recorded as a witch who died by burning.

Burning was considered a woman's penalty, having regard to the decency of the sex. Public mangling of a woman's body was forbidden, so women convicted of murder, treason or heresy were burnt alive. In the case of witches, many were hanged first, and their bodies then burnt, this being regarded as a sure way of ridding the place of witch-like influences. Burning as a penalty for treason remained a Common Law penalty until 1790.

None of the North York Moors witches was, to my knowledge, hanged or imprisoned for practising her art even though a law passed in 1736 made it illegal, albeit not a capital offence, to pretend to practise any kind of witchcraft, sorcery, enchantment or conjuration. There was a prosecution under this Act as late as 1904 (*R.v. Stephenson*) and in 1939, a gipsy was prosecuted at Portsmouth for unlawfully undertaking to tell fortunes and remove a spell! That law remained on our statute book until 1951.

On the North York Moors, there could be a mystery element in the manner in which stories of witchcraft have persisted in these remote areas. Why, for example, are the witch-hare tales so strong, with elements persisting until just before the Second World War? What is the purpose of the witch posts, examples of which can still be seen in moorland cottages and museums? Of the witch posts known to exist, all but one were found on the North York Moors, the odd one being in Lancashire.

The North York Moors witches were not made in the traditional image of a witch; there were no pointed hats and broomsticks, no naked moonlight rituals, no covens in woodlands or by secret waterways, no sabbats or devil-worshipping. Instead, they were ladies of indeterminate age who lived in small villages. The good and wise dabbled in herbal and mystical cures for both humans and livestock. They also offered advice on a wide range of problems, often aided by the knowledge of portents, herbs and curious rituals. They were probably the agony aunts of their time.

The evil ones, on the other hand, operated in secret and caused diseases, upsets, sickness and a whole range of other nuisances to people, places, plants, animals and buildings. Feared by the simple folk, the blame for these ailments was often placed upon deformed or ugly old women who lived alone and who were probably simpletons or odd in some way. As long ago as 1599, the

Archbishop of York, Simon Harsnett, described a witch as, 'an old weather-beaten crone, having her chin and her knees meeting for age, walking like a bow, leaning on a staff, hollow-eyed, untoothed, furrowed on her face, having limbs trembling with palsy, going mumbling in the streets and hath a shrewd tongue.' Another description was, 'old, lame, bleary eyed, pale, foul and full of wrinkles', while one account says, 'There are more women than men because women have a slippery tongue and tell other women what they have learned.'

Old Mother Shipton, the Knaresborough prophetess and witch, was born Ursula Sontheil in 1488, the daughter of a woman convicted of practising witchcraft. This is a description of her: 'The body was long, but very big boned, great goggling eyes, very sharp and fiery, a nose of unproportionate length, having in it many crooks and turnings adorned with pimples.' She also had crooked, misshapen legs.

Not all witches were old or deformed, however. Isobel Gowdie, aged only eighteen, admitted being a witch and was hanged in Scotland, her body afterwards being burnt to ashes, while one in Germany, aged nineteen, was described as 'the fairest maid in Wurtzburg'.

Nonetheless, deformed old women were generally identified as witches, especially if they had the misfortune to live and operate during the highly superstitious medieval times and even well into the seventeenth and eighteenth centuries. Even noted people believed in witches, devils and demons. For example, the famous scholar, Johan Weyer (1515-88) claimed he had counted all the devils in hell and found 7,405,926 demons and seventy-two princes of hell. There's little doubt others believed his word.

In the remote moors, superstition and the fear it generated, continued until well into the last century; memories of witches and their associated rituals extended even into the first quarter of this century.

Within living memory, superstition was extremely strong upon the moors for it replaced, or was sometimes combined with, religion and a limited medical knowledge for beast and man. The service offered by good witches was performed by men and women, the men becoming known as wise men while the women were wise women. The evil ones were regarded as witches and they greatly outnumbered wise men and wise women. These beliefs were particularly strong in the area around Whitby and in Eskdale, albeit with similar ideas circulating other areas. The beliefs were not restricted to the simple, lowly and ignorant classes. Farmers and other livestock-holders were especially worried about witches as they struggled to keep their beasts free from harm. For them, healthy livestock were vital to their own survival, and in the absence of modern veterinary services, all manner of dubious charms were exercised to ensure the good health and breeding potential of their animals. A tremendous amount of witch lore concerns livestock and farm crops. The good witches offered advice for curers while the evil ones cast the 'evil eye'; this made the milk go sour, prevented the cheese from turning or the dough from rising; it made animals impotent or ill, or crops to fail and it caused a whole range of other problems which we would regard as bad luck or minor misfortunes. But for the superstitious folk, such annoyances were the work of bad witches and they sought means of preventing them.

The following is perhaps a good example of the kind of witchcraft which worried the moorland folk and the efforts made to stamp it out. In 1840, the vicar of Nunnington near Kirkbymoorside, the Revd Keary, learned from his daughter, Anne, that some cows in the village had died. The villagers believed the animals had been bewitched by a local witch who had bought a cow's heart, pricked it with pins while quoting a verse, and then burnt it. One cow which had died was examined in a post-mortem and it was discovered that its heart was full of holes, so enforcing the belief that it was the work of a witch. A wise woman was called in to trace the witch so that steps could be taken to stop her evil ways. When the Revd Keary heard this, he asked the farmer to do his best among his workers to dismiss the notion that a witch had been involved. He was probably surprised by the farmer's response which was, 'You may be wise, parson, and I know you are learned, but in this case you are mistaken. It's a matter you know nothing about, you're sadly wrong. I saw it with my own eyes.'

At Goathland, a village high on the moors above Whitby, a man who tried to prevent evil spells with a bullock's heart pierced with pins and concealed in a chimney, died as recently as 1926. The belief was that as the heart dried and withered, so would that of the witch who had caused the trouble. Some of these wizened old hearts have been found during alterations to country cottages.

Over the centuries, the superstitious people adopted a bewildering array of other practices which were designed to ward off evil spirits or bad luck. In those times, any misfortune, but especially illness in people or animals and failure of crops, was considered the result of either witch-craft, the evil eye or the machinations of other imps and devils. Nowadays, illness is readily explained and treated, but many of those other worries, once regarded as the work of the evil eye, witches or the devil, are interpreted simply as bad luck or they could be due to bad organization or poor skills.

Upon the North York Moors and indeed elsewhere, evidence remains of the attempts to keep such evil influences at bay. One of the best examples is the horseshoe. Even today, it signifies good luck, a fact which is clearly evident at most weddings as the bride is presented with a symbolic horseshoe. But horseshoes adorn the walls of farmhouses, cottages and outbuildings of the North York Moors as they have for centuries, their purpose being to keep away witches or evil spirits.

This practice dates to the time when iron, in any form, was thought to keep witches and evil spirits at bay. A nail in the woodwork of a bed, especially that of a woman about to give birth, or in the frame of a baby's cot, or in the beams of a roof or doorway, was placed there to ward off evil. Some women hid scissors under beds or cushions, or kept iron objects about the house and in the dairy.

For the exterior walls and outbuildings, discarded iron horseshoes were ideal. Some buildings around the moors have doorways shaped like horseshoes – there is a fine example at Upsall near Thirsk. But other charms were used to ward off witches, some placed upon the animals such as the elaborately carved brasses worn by horses or the sprigs of rowan (mountain ash) which adorned some cattle. Around the houses and farms, elderberry trees were planted, simple crosses were fashioned from hazelwood for urgent protection, some buildings were decorated with circular stones with a hole in the centre, glass globes were hung in windows, corn dollies were created from harvested corn, or witch-bottles were buried under thresholds. These were sealed jars containing gruesome contents such as hair, human nail-cuttings, iron nails, blood or urine. In every case, the charm was designed to keep away witches.

But the most intriguing of protective charms are the witch posts. These can still be seen, for the largest known (and maybe the only) assembly is found upon these Moors. A witch post is an upright piece of stout, seasoned timber, usually of oak but perhaps of rowan. It forms part of the structure of a house. Sometimes it supports one end of the smoke hood of a cottage, and its purpose can be identified by a crude cross which is carved into its face near the top. Some are nothing more than a simple X, while others have symbols around the X. Some contain dates, one being 1664; there are initials and other carvings from the seventeenth century.

A fine example can be seen in Ryedale Folk Museum at

Hutton-le-Hole on the North York Moors where it has been incorporated into a reconstructed cottage after being removed from a house at Danby. Although they are called witch posts and it is assumed their purpose was to ward off witches, there is no firm evidence to support this. Oddly, there are only nineteen known examples and all but one have come from the North York Moors, the exception being a post from Rawtenstall in Lancashire. In 1984, a cottage at Newton-on-Rawcliffe near Pickering was sold, and one of its features was a witch post. Others are known at Glaisdale, Rosedale, Gillamoor, Farndale, Egton and Lealholm and two near Scarborough. Today, some of the existing witch posts can be seen in the Pitt-Rivers Museum, Oxford, the Ryedale Folk Museum and the Whitby Museum, with the others remaining in cottages which are still in occupation around the Moors.

One theory is that visiting priests blessed the cottages in question to protect them and their residents against witches, the occasion being permanently marked by the carving of a cross on these wooden uprights. Maybe they were the mark of just one travelling priest? If this is so, would Father Postgate (*see* Chapter 5) have known of these posts? They were created in his time. But maybe they are nothing to do with witches? Together, these nineteen curious posts present just one of the mysteries of the North York Moors.

Prominent among the stories of the Moors are the witch-hare tales. Over the centuries, these have been told with such force and honesty that they survive into modern times. Although this kind of story, where a witch turns into the form of an animal, goes back into the mists of time with many variations on the type of animal, there is one account of a Yorkshire farm labourer asking for a damaged sixpence with which to shoot a witch who had taken the form of a dog. She was bothering the sheep and he wanted to shoot the animal; he knew the only thing that would kill it was a bullet made from silver, hence the request for a damaged sixpence. The surprising thing is that this happened just before the Second World War, only some fifty years ago.

In the moors, the surviving stories tell how local witches turned themselves into hares. Each tale followed a similar pattern; a hunt puts up a hare and there is a long chase. The hare runs for its life until it reaches an old barn or cottage where there is a hole in the wall or door. At this stage, a hound manages to seize the hare, injuring its leg, or else it is injured by one of the huntsmen with a shotgun. But it escapes through the hole into the locked barn or cottage, albeit injured. Very shortly afterwards, a local woman who lives there and who is known to be a witch, is seen with injuries corresponding to those inflicted upon the hare.

Isobel Gowdie, the eighteen-year-old Scottish witch mentioned earlier, claimed in 1662 that she could turn herself into a hare. But the belief goes back to ancient times, when fear led people to assume their fellows could become werewolves, cats, dogs, bears and other beasts. It's a theme which has been used in fiction too, as in Bram Stoker's *Dracula* where the infamous count raced up Whitby's famous 199 steps in the form of a dog.

Here on the Moors, however, there remain witch-hare accounts which have links with modern times. I repeat them here, not because there is any truth in them, but because they form part of the centuries-old mystique which surrounds rural life on the North York Moors.

One well-known, oft-told but somewhat exaggerated tale concerns Peg Humphrey of East Moors, near Helmsley. It involves Bobby Dowson who was a famous Bilsdale hunts-man, a member of England's oldest fox-hunt. He died in 1902, aged eighty-six, and his memorial stone can be seen at the Sun Inn, Bilsdale, beside the B1257 (Helmsley-to-Stokesley road). He told this story to Major J. Fairfax-Blakeborough, the Yorkshire author, who died in 1976, aged ninety-three. In turn, the Major told it to me in a letter.

Around 1860, when Bobby was about forty-four, he and

some friends were hunting hares and they put up one which made straight for Peg's home at East Moors. It vanished through a hole in the barn door.

The men followed and opened the door to find Peg lying on the straw, panting heavily. 'I've been foddering', she gasped, 'the door blew shut.' On another occasion, Bobby Dowson chased a hare towards Peg's home and the hounds managed to nip a piece of flesh and fur from a leg. The injured hare continued its run and 'ran straight through Peg's house end'. When the hunters entered the house, they found Peg lying on her bed, exhausted and injured on the same leg as the hare.

They took her to a doctor in Helmsley and it was said she was lame for life. However, I also have an account from the late Bill Agar Weatherill, the grandson of a personal friend of Peg. He says, 'Peg Humphrey was reputed by some to be a witch, but she was a personal friend of my grandmother and she was no witch. When she came over into the dale, she would call and have a drink o' tea with my granny.'

So how do such tales originate?

There is another one concerning the Guisborough witch, Jane Grear, who was bitten by a dog while galloping in the form of a hare, and Peggy Flaunders of Marske-by-the-Sea who was also hunted as a hare and bitten on the haunch. She died in 1835. Jane Wood was a witch-hare who lived in Baysdale, while Nan Hardwicke who lived near Danby, would let the local lads flush her out with dogs, but they never caught her.

There is an account of Nan visiting a relation in Farndale which was over ten miles away, and changing herself into a hare to speed her journey. Nanny Pearson of Goathland could also turn herself into a hare but was shot by the man who was courting the squire's daughter; he used a silver bullet, but the hare was not killed. Nan was seen next day with corresponding injuries.

On one occasion, the hare turned on the hunter! Awd

Mally, a Westerdale witch, turned herself into a hare and was stealing milk when a farmer, with his shotgun full of silver shot made from old buttons, aimed his gun at her. But the hare attacked him and he fled; an account says: 'She cem at him wiv her een glooring and widening while they were as big as saucers.'

But if there is a favourite witch-hare story of mine, it is the one which occurred at Glaisdale where I was born, a village rich with moorland legends and romance. High in the dale which leads from Glaisdale End into the moors, there came a report that 'no mere ordinary hare' was biting the tops off some young saplings which had been planted near the dale head. The angry farmer decided to lay in wait and shoot it. Knowing that this might be a witch-hare, he made some bullets from his silver buttons and loaded these into his firearm. Then he concealed himself near his nursery and waited.

At the witching hour of midnight, the hare appeared and these are the farmer's words,

> It was a greeat foul awd ram-cat of a heear, an' it began knepping here and knepping there. It wur stoodying how best ti deea t'maist ill in t'lahlest tahme. Sae t'chap at wur watching (himself!), well, he up wiv his gun and aiming steady, let dhrive. My wod, but there was a flaysome shrike! At that, t'heear, sair hot, gat hersel' a sooart o' croppen oot o' t'nossery and hoppled away as wheel as she could and gat heeam at Aud Maggie's house-end, in a bit o' scroggs at grows on t'bank there.

Aud Maggie was a reputed witch and when the rough land (scroggs) was searched, nothing was found, but the following day she was found in bed with severe injuries; she said she had fallen on some broken glass.

These tales were told around the firesides of the dark country cottages and helped to perpetuate the superstitious fears which were bred into the moorland folk. I was brought up on such tales but accepted them as stories from the past, not necessarily true.

But for anyone wishing to pursue the tales of witches within the North York Moors, the Ryedale Folk Museum has a treasure-trove of information and artefacts, including a hovel containing a model witch. The children love her. Some of the wise men of the moors are known to have come from these villages and market towns – Byland, Kilburn, Nunnington, Helmsley, Kirkbymoorside, Lastingham, Cropton and Scarborough.

The most famous was John Wrightson, the wise man of Stokesley. People travelled from every corner of the moors to obtain his advice and to benefit from his powers of clairvoyance, and he travelled widely to meet them too. He claimed he was the seventh son of a seventh son and advertised his services, offering cures for sick people and animals, help with finding lost or stolen goods and even advice on the problems of love or the removal of curses. He seems to have made a reasonable living, but for some reason, in 1808, he fled from Stokesley to Malton. He lived in Newbiggin 'having made Cleveland too hot to hold him' and then, in 1818, he was arrested. I am not sure of his crime, but he was taken to Northallerton prison and as the horse-drawn prison vehicle was passing through Hovingham, John Wrightson poisoned himself.

If the names of the other wisemen are not known, then the names of many witches have survived. Lots are prefixed by the word 'aud' or 'awd', which is the North Riding dialect term for 'old.' It does not necessary mean aged, however, but is more often a term of respect or even affection.

At Goathland, there was a witch called Nan or Nanny Pearson (sometimes spelt Pierson), one of three of that name; one lived into this century and another was said to turn herself into a hare as stated earlier. There is a tale of one Nanny Pearson being hit by a stick, and the man then felt a pain and found a hare-shaped footmark on his chest.

On another occasion, a lady called Mrs Richardson who died in 1940 aged eighty-three told how, as a child at Goathland, she had seen Nanny Pearson grow smaller and smaller until she disappeared into a crockery cupboard to walk around among the contents. The witch had boasted she could do that, and was described as, 'sitting in a corner clad in a dress of blue and white check that fell in folds around her. She had a huge flap bonnet on, so only her nose and a clay pipe as long as a poker protruded.'

Other witches included Awd Molly Milburn of Danby who was noted for her cures, Betty Strother who lived 'ower by Castleton' and was known for her love potions, and Awd Mother Migg from Lastingham who used a magic looking-glass, a crystal ball and sold sigills and other charms. Sigills are talismans and can be seen in Ryedale Folk Museum.

Among the other witches are Awd Kathy o' Ruswarp, Awd Nan Scaife o' Spaunton Moor who used a magic cube, Sally Craggs o' Allerston who could change into a cat, Esther Mudd o' Rosedale who used the evil eye, Emma Todd o' Ebberston who was well versed in the black arts, Nancy Nairs o' Pickering who used a crystal, Peggy Devell o' Hutton-le-Hole who used a magic book, Awd Jennie o' Mulgrave who terrified local people with her spells and incantations, and Awd Mally o' Westerdale who could turn into a hare.

So when you perform a little act for good luck, think of these witches and the methods used to keep them at bay. Like cracking the shell of a boiled egg after eating it ...

7　Unexplained Tales from the Moors

This chapter is devoted to four unsolved mysteries which, through the passage of time and a lack of evidence, will never be positively determined. The first and indeed the oldest is widely known, so much so that its legacy has become a focus of interest for tourists. The other stories may be less well known but are of equal interest.

Who killed the Hermit of Eskdale?

Who was the Hermit of Eskdale and who killed him?

The death of the hermit of Eskdale is still comme-morated at Whitby by a curious ritual which is witnessed by foreign visitors, sightseers and journalists. The brief ceremony follows this pattern; at 9 a.m. on the eve of every Ascension Day, a small party gathers on the mud of the upper harbour at Whitby. They are suitably dressed in wellington boots, for the mud is thick and sticky, but one holds a horn while two others carry bundles of small pliable branches and twigs.

Some of the sticks are planted upright in the mud and others are then woven between them to create a short length of fencing. When this is done, the horn is sounded and the blower calls, 'Out on ye, out on ye, out on ye.' What should be called is, 'Out on ye, out on ye, out on ye *for this heinous crime.*' The heinous crime was in fact a vicious murder when three men attacked the hermit/monk with boar staves. He died later from his injuries.

Featured in Sir Walter Scott's *Marmion*, the crime occurred on 16 October 1159 in the fifth year of the reign of King Henry II. Three men decided to hunt wild boar and they have been named as Ralph de Percy, the Lord of Sneaton, William de Brus, the Lord of Ugglebarnby and a mutual friend and freeholder of Fylingdales called Allatson. The family of de Brus were massive property-owners in the north of England including parts of Eskdale. At this time, Adam de Brus held Castleton Castle and the Lordship of Danby. The family were founders of Guisborough Priory and ancestors or Robert the Bruce, the King of Scotland who was famed for the determination he engendered through watching a spider attempting to make a web. The de Percy family was equally well known and owned lands in the Whitby area as well as some hundred other manors. The Percys became Earls of Northumberland, with Sir Henry (1366-1403) being known as Hotspur, a name made famous by Shakespeare. The families were related through marriage. In addition one of the abbots at Whitby was William de Percy and a prior at Guisborough was William de Brus. Allatson, on the other hand, is not well known, although persons of this name did occupy land at Robin Hood's Bay.

The place selected for hunting wild boar by these three young men was a patch of land close to the River Esk near Sleights. It belonged to Whitby Abbey and was then heavily forested. Living in the forest, in a small chapel beside the river, was a hermit who was also a monk of Whitby Abbey. The site of that chapel is about a mile upstream from Sleights railway station, on the Sleights side of the Esk.

In the forest, the hunters and their dogs put up a huge wild boar which fled for its life. Then followed a period of drama and this amended account is said to be taken from the original tale, dated AD 1160:

The boar, being sore [wounded and hotly] pursued, and dead-run, took in at the Chapel-door and there laid him down, and presently died. The Hermit shut the hounds forth of the Chapel and kept himself within at his Meditation and Prayers, the hounds standing at bay without. The Gentlemen in the Thick of the Wood, put behind their Game, following the Cry of the Hounds, came to the Hermitage, and found the Hounds round about the Chapel. Then came the Gentlemen to the Door of the Chapel and called the Hermit, who did open the door and come forth, and within the boar lay dead. For which the Gentlemen, in a Fury, because the Hounds were put from their Game, did [most violently and cruelly], run at the Hermit with their boar staves, whereof he died.

But he did not die immediately; the hunters, shocked at what they had done, fled to sanctuary at Scarborough, while the hermit managed to call for help. Knowing his injuries would be fatal, he asked the Abbot of Whitby Abbey to visit him and to bring his attackers too. They thought that his death would result in their own execution, but, being a man of God, he persuaded them to come by asking them if they would, instead of death, be agreeable to a penance.

Knowing the hermit had saved their lives, they agreed to this and visited him along with the abbot. Before them all, the dying hermit said this:

Upon Ascension Eve, you or some of you, shall come to the Wood of the Strayhead which is in Eskdaleside, the same Day at sun-rising, and there shall the officer of the Abbot blow his horn, to the intent that you may know how to find him, and he shall deliver unto you, William de Brus, ten stakes, ten stout-bowers and ten yedders, to be cut by you, or those that come after you, with a knife of a Penny price; and you, Ralph de Piercie, shall take one and twenty of each sort to be cut in the same manner; and you Allatson, shall take nine of each sort, to be cut as aforesaid.

And to be taken on your backs and carried to the town of Whitby and so to be there before nine of the Clock (if it be full sea, to cease Service), as long as it is low water at nine of the Clock, the same hour each of you shall set your stakes at the Brim of the water, each stake a yard from another, and so yedder them, as with Yedders, and so stake on each side with your stout-bowers, that they stand Three Tides without removing by the Force of the Water. Each of you shall make them in several places at the hour above-named (except it to be full sea at that hour, which when it shall happen to pass, that Service shall cease), and you shall do this service in remembrance that you did (most) cruelly slay me.

He went on,

And that you may the better call to God for Repentance, and find Mercy, and do good Works, the Officer of Eskdaleside shall blow his horn Out on You, Out on You for the heinous crime of You. And if you, and your Successors, do refuse this service, so long as it shall not be at full sea at that hour, you and yours shall forfeit all your land to the Abbot of Whitby or his successors.

As a matter of interest, the wild boar became extinct in this country around three hundred years ago, the last in the north reputedly being killed in Stuart times on Wild Boar Fell high in the Yorkshire Dales. And yedders are young pliable branches which are woven horizontally through upright stakes to make a fence.

Having imposed this fence-making chore upon his attackers, the hermit died on 18 December, two months after the assault and the men began their penance. In 1305, there was a dispute between Sir Alexander de Percy of Sneaton, a grandson of the elder William de Percy of Kildale and the then abbot of Whitby, Thomas de Malton.

It concerned the method of performing the ceremony, but the problem was resolved and the Planting of the Penny Hedge continues to this day.

Also known as the Horngarth Ceremony, it varies slightly from the format imposed by the hermit but in a period extending over more than eight hundred years, this is not surprising. The basic ritual has, however, been retained.

The hermit wanted a horn to be blown in the wood – this no longer happens; the knife must, due to inflation, now cost more than one penny, and during the modern planting ceremony there is no reference to 'the heinous crime'. And always, over the centuries, it has been possible to plant the hedge at 9 a.m. on Ascension Eve because, until 1981, there had never at that time been a high tide (or a full sea as the hermit described it).

So how did a simple hermit know that the tide would never cover that piece of mud at 9 a.m. on Ascension Eve, even though the date of Ascension Eve varies considerably from year to year, as do the times of the high tides? The planting has continued for more than 820 years but then in 1981, things did change. On the Eve of the Ascension, which fell on 27 May that year, a freak tide covered the mud to a depth of eight feet. It was impossible to plant the Penny Hedge and so this brought to an end the years of penance imposed on the three hunters and their successors for committing their 'heinous crime.' But, as a matter of custom, the penance will continue. As a penalty for a crime, it must surely be one of the longest duration.

But over those centuries, there is doubt about its authenticity. When the Whitby historian Lionel Charlton researched the story around 1779, he could not prove that men of that name existed in the Whitby area at that time, nor that the abbey possessed any documents relating to the agreement of this penance by the abbot and the landowners.

Neither is proof that the tale is untrue, however. Men of that name might have lived there without us having documentary proof of the fact; documents relating to the land deal might have been lost or destroyed. Although we do not know whether those men actually lived or whether the Abbey authorities agreed to the curious penance, the 1305 dispute between the de Percy family and the Abbot of Whitby Abbey does add some credibility to the story.

So was there, after all, a murder? It is known that several monks occupied that lonely chapel near Sleights, for it had been built as a place of solitude and devotion for the monks of Whitby Abbey who needed some time on their own. One such monk was Godric, and in an account of his life there, we learn that he was 'frequently molested' and that he found the place 'unpleasing'; there is also a story that he gave sanctuary to a hunted stag. Another monk who supposedly lived there was Brother Jerome and one account suggests that he was the victim of that murder. That he was a man of standing and intelligence may be suggested by the fact that he was none other than Sir Richard de Veron, a distinguished knight who held considerable lands through his service with the famous de Brus family from Guisborough. He was a hero of the Battle of the Standard at Northallerton in 1138, and fought many valiant battles for his king and country. At the end of his fighting career, Sir Richard retired to Guisborough with his beloved wife and two children, but tragically, they caught the plague.

His entire family was wiped out and so devastated was he that he sought solace in the church, eventually becoming a monk of Whitby Abbey. To overcome his grievous family loss, and to atone for his own past life of violence and fighting, Sir Richard, now known as Brother Jerome, asked to be permitted the life of a hermit in the little chapel at Sleights. There, he wanted to spend a life in prayer in an effort to atone for his own life of violence and killing, albeit as a professional soldier.

One must wonder whether, if this is true, his death was perhaps due not to the sheltering of a boar, but to some other deep-seated feud among the landowners of the time? After all, one of the killers was a member of the de Brus family and, with Sir Richard having no heirs, maybe William de Brus could see this as a way of obtaining Sir Richard's estates? We can speculate that de Brus was worried in case Sir Richard, upon his eventual ordination as a priest, handed over his lands to the church? Maybe the attack in the wood was nothing more than scare tactics, an effort to persuade Sir Richard against becoming an ordained monk so that his lands might be transferred to the de Brus family? Is the tale of a fleeing boar nothing more than a cover-up, a story to make their strange attack appear more acceptable?

We shall never know, but at 9 a.m. on the eve of every Ascension Day, the death of that anonymous hermit/monk is still remembered as modern families pay the penance for a heinous crime committed more than 820 years ago.

Kings and a Con Man at Allerston?

Allerston is a tiny but pretty village just off the A170 road between Pickering and Scarborough, and it lies about five miles from Pickering. The main road slices across the northern tip of the village, consequently a visit to Allerston means a short but very pleasant diversion although the local inn, the Cayley Arms Hotel, is conveniently situated on the main road at this junction. In the village, the small, aisleless church justifies a visit.

It seems odd that such a tiny community should be the location of not one, but two royal mysteries; one involves a killing and the other an attempted deal involving a horse.

On the hills to the north are the famous Scamridge Dykes, an extensive and remarkable series of ancient ditches and mounds, the remains of a prehistoric settlement. During the last century, the remains of a communal thatched dwelling and fourteen skeletons were found and were dated to around 1000 BC. It was on these hills that a mystery killing is said to have occurred; the site is known today as Bloody Field, while Alfred's Cave, which is among the earthworks, is a reminder of that ancient death.

It was here that King Aldfrith of Northumbria (685-704) fought his father, King Oswy, at the Battle of Ebberston. Aldfrith was severely stabbed and sheltered in a rocky cave which has since been known as Aldfrith's Cave, or Alfred's Cave. The mystery remains as to whether or not he actually died here.

Some accounts suggest that he did while another account by no less an authority than the Venerable Bede, believes he survived the wounds received at Scamridge and died later from natural causes in Driffield. The date has been given as 14 December AD 704.

But this royal mystery is not the only one to linger in this village. The second concerned an alleged visit by King Charles II, and this tale continues to feature in the folklore of the area where support for the Royalist cause was very strong. It is said that the Cayley Arms Hotel at Allerston sheltered the King, although it was not known by that name at the time. It is a sad fact that so little is recorded in writing about this inn before 1810.

Nonetheless, stories of the King's visit do continue to circulate in the form of folk memory, and the story began when a man called Robert Awderson was riding his horse between Allerston and Ebberston. The year was 1656, and the time was about two weeks before Christmas. We are not told where Awderson was heading, nor the purpose of his journey, but during this short trip he met a traveller called Matthew Vasey. Vasey was a local man who lived at Marishes, a few miles distant and to the south of Pickering.

As they stopped and chatted, Vasey admired

Awderson's horse, a fine grey gelding and suddenly surprised Awderson by saying that if he would give the horse to King Charles, he would be paid £500 in due course.

In those times, the normal price for a horse was about £10, consequently this was a staggering offer. Vasey went on to say that three men had travelled from Bridlington, one of whom was Charles II, and they had passed through Ebberston two days earlier. They had then gone to a house in Allerston 'to lye downe on a bedde there and gett some potchett (poached eggs)'. Having rested overnight and eaten, the King and his two companions had departed yesterday, travelling northwards upon horses which they had obtained for £10 each. But it seemed the King required a better horse, hence the approach to Awderson.

The outcome of the deal involving the grey gelding is not known. To the suspicious mind of a police officer, it sounds like a typical confidence trick, a means of attempting to obtain a horse by deception. It involves the old plot of obtaining goods with a promise to pay handsomely at a later time. Many have succumbed to this type of promise, the snag being that payment is never made. I wonder if Awderson did part with his horse upon the promise of that £500; after all, it was, by any standards, a colossal sum of money and must have been very tempting.

We do not know whether he believed the tale about the King or whether it is true that the King ever visited Allerston to sleep and eat poached eggs. This is a genuine mystery, but it is claimed that the place in question was the inn, now known as the Cayley Arms Hotel. That the King should select an inn for his stay is very feasible.

But the date presents a problem. Awderson's encounter with Vasey occurred in December 1656; that date has been confirmed by depositions heard at York Assizes and it rules out King Charles I as the sovereign in question. He had been executed in 1649 by the Puritans. Cromwell had become Lord Protector of England and he held that office at the time of Vasey's bid for Awderson's horse. At the time, Charles II was in exile, doing his best to stay alive and attempting by various means to muster support so that he could regain his Crown. History tells us that he fled to the continent in 1654. He did this in the hope that he could open successful negotiations with the governments of several countries, as he struggled to restore himself as King of England. These efforts were not successful, although he gained a boost for his morale when he was crowned King of Scotland in 1651. In 1654, Cromwell's negotiations with France compelled Charles to go to Germany, but it is known that after Cromwell's alliance with France, Charles made a treaty with Spain.

That occurred in April 1656, only eight months before Vasey's offer to Awderson and we know that Charles was desperately short of money, his only income being a meagre pension from Spain. When Cromwell died in 1658, Charles was on the continent, and in 1659, he went to Fuenterrabia, where the Peace of the Pyrenees was being negotiated between France and Spain, to ask for military aid. His efforts were fruitless. So he spent a long time out of England.

Richard Cromwell succeeded his father as Lord Protector in 1658, but resigned in 1659 when the Commonwealth was re-established. The monarchy was restored in 1660, and Charles II regained the throne to become King of England, Scotland and Ireland.

The mystery is whether, in December 1656, the exiled Charles II was actively seeking the help of continental governments in his battle for restoration as King of England, or whether he was eating poached eggs at Allerston.

If he was in Allerston at that time, the history books are wrong, although his visit might have been one of great secrecy. Perhaps he was recruiting English help for his return to the throne, operating in this country in heavy disguise while Cromwell's government thought he was overseas? That is a strong possibility. Certainly, he had friends in and near Allerston. The Cayley family at nearby Brompton were strong supporters of the Royalist cause and there were many more in the surrounding district.

But can history rely on the word of Matthew Vasey that the King had slept overnight at Allerston and eaten poached eggs when everyone thought he was overseas, or was this tale nothing more than part of a confidence trick through which Vasey would acquire a fine grey gelding without paying for it?

The Bride in the Oak Chest

No collection of mystery stories would be complete without the traditional tale of The Bride in the Oak Chest and the Moors do have their own Bride in the Chest story. It follows the traditional pattern. A beautiful and wealthy girl called Frances Lovell was married to a handsome landowner, and the nuptial celebrations took place in her fabulous home. This was a lovely and historic mansion and the party continued until dawn. Before it broke up, the guests decided they would have a game of hide-and-seek, and the first 'away' should be the bride.

Off went Frances to hide as the others remained in the Drawing-Room and counted slowly up to one hundred. Then the search began. The searchers hunted all night … no one found the bride. The guests, the extremely anxious bridegroom and the couples' parents expressed grave concern, and all the staff were called into assist. Had she run away? Had she fallen? Was she lying injured in the grounds?

A full-scale and thorough search was organized, with the stables being checked for stolen horses, the carts and coaches being inspected, along with all the known hiding-places in the grounds and within the spacious building. The dungeons, the cellars, the priest holes within the stout walls, the attics – everywhere was checked and re-checked, then checked again.

But the missing Frances was never found alive.

Unknown to her family, friends and guests, Frances had concealed herself in the huge oak chest which stood in the entrance hall. Gently, she had lowered the massive, heavy lid until she lay securely hidden in the darkness, but after a long, long time, no one found her. So she tried to get out. But the weight of the heavy stout metal clasp had caused it to hook itself over the hesp. The lid was firmly closed and she could not lift it; it could only be opened from the outside. She beat upon the lid with her fists, she shouted and screamed for help, but the thick timbers and the general noise of the party obliterated all her cries.

Utterly puzzled, the household abandoned the search, and the bridegroom thought his precious Frances had been carried off by another jealous suitor. And so the terrible wedding party ended with sadness. The groom never found his bride.

Many, many years later, a completely new generation of occupants explored the old mansion and discovered the chest. With some curiosity, one of them opened the lid and there inside were the dry bones of a young woman, still wrapped in the remains of her wedding dress. The discovery led to stories of murder, of ghosts and of suicide, but someone then uncovered the sad story of Frances Lovell.

But where did this happen? One account suggests it was at Skelton Castle in Cleveland, and another felt it might be an early Skelton Manor near York. But no one knows and so we must regard the story as nothing more than a sad ballad. It is one of those ballads which have for centuries, albeit in slightly different forms, been told over log fires to the entertainment or perhaps the horror of household guests, family members and visitors. There are many country houses, inns and castle which claim such a tale, and I have been in several of them. One tale of this kind even surrounds a massive chest which stands in the entrance hall of the Police Staff College at the magnificent and historic Bramshill House near Basingstoke in Hampshire.

Most of these tales relate to premises which are open to the public, consequently they become part of the local folklore and the chest in which the bride suffocated or starved to death becomes an object of macabre tourist interest. It is part of the marketing of the place and I'm sure several of these tales have been created especially for tourism. But this is not the case with the Bramshill chest, nor is it the case with a chest upon the North York Moors, for the suggested premises are not open to the public.

There is, incidentally, a mysterious chest at Danby Castle deep within the Moors, but this does not contain a corpse; for generations, its multiple locks secured the lid so that rumours about its possible contents circulated in the area.

It was opened in the 1980s, an act which confirmed that it held nothing more exciting or dramatic than old papers and ancient deeds of the local Court Leet and Baron, a court which continues to function as it administers rights of way and common land.

Who killed Henry Edwards?

A small area near Stokesley has suffered a large tally of murders for such a pleasant and compact rural district. One was the murder of Anthony Noble, who was killed in a close near Great Broughton. His brother-in-law, William Parkin, was found guilty of this crime and sentenced to death at York Assizes. Parkin was brought back from York, had a hefty lunch of beef and potatoes at the Three Tuns in Stokesley, and was then hanged and gibbeted on the edge of Ingleby Greenhow. The date was Friday 15 August 1729, but as the gibbet offended the view by the Foulis family who occupied Ingleby Manor, it was removed.

A few years later, in 1753, three more murders occurred at Ingleby Greenhow. William Smith poisoned his brother-in-law, Thomas Harper, and Harper's two children, William and Annie. He did so by poisoning them with arsenic. Knowing they enjoyed a Good Friday Cake on this holy day, he bought some arsenic from a shop in Great Ayton, and mixed it with the flour which would be used to make the cake. The family consumed the cake and died.

Smith was not suspected of any crime until, on Easter Sunday, he absconded with the intention of travelling to Ireland. The story of his purchase at Great Ayton then emerged; in the meantime, Smith had reached Liverpool but for some reason, changed his mind and returned to Ingleby, only to be arrested for murder.

He was tried on Monday 13 August at York Assizes, found guilty and sentenced to death. He was executed the following Wednesday on the gallows outside Micklegate Bar, York. Before going to his death, he wrote to his wife, pleading with her to consider re-marriage to 'young farmer Alcock's son', whom she courted before her marriage to Smith. As he wrote, 'Marry him and carry on the farm, and as my son grows up, pray do not let him know there was such an unhappy person as I am. Walk in the paths of virtue and sobriety, go to church and mind what is good. You know I did not love to go to church, but see what has now become of it.'

His motive for the murders was to secure his father-in-law's farm for his growing family.

These murders, like so many domestic ones, were quickly solved, but there is a curious tale of another at Stokesley which, for a time, remained unsolved. The story begins in 1830 at Anngrove Hall, the Manor House at Stokesley which is a fine market town at the northern edge of the North York Moors. The under-coachman was called Henry Edwards and he became the lover of the daughter of the house. The couple even became engaged, but the moment the girl's father heard of their romance, he tried to put a stop to it. He forbade them seeing one another, but quite understandably, found some strong resistance from both parties. The reason for her father's objection is not known, although the difference in the social class of the lovers may have been a factor.

Not long afterwards, the girl's father called his butler and asked him if Henry Edwards had returned from Stokesley. He had apparently been sent there with a box of valuable silver plate and jewellery which he was to hand over to a gentlemen travelling to London by coach. The butler said Edwards had not returned, and so the master issued orders that the moment he did return, he was to speak with the master. The butler promised to pass on the instruction.

When it was clear that Edwards was not going to return, the master claimed he had stolen the valuables and made off with the proceeds. He ordered his coach, jumped on board and drove all the way to Thirsk where he spent the day making enquiries. He even offered a reward of £200 for the arrest of the thief. But no one had seen Edwards, although everyone showed shock when it was learned he had betrayed the trust of his master and the household.

The story went around that Edwards, still in love with the master's daughter, had been unable to live up to her family's expectations, and had therefore stolen the silver and jewellery in an attempt to raise some money. Months then passed with no trace of the missing man, and his absence faded in the memories of the local people. But it did not fade in the mind of Edwards' sister, Polly.

She was a servant at The Grange, Great Ayton, a large house only two miles away, and she firmly believed that her brother would never have committed such a crime.

So sure was she of his innocence, that she asked the Anngrove Hall coachman for a shoe from Nancy, one of the horses her brother used to drive and his special favourite. These country folk lived in very superstitious times and she took the shoe to a woman who lived at Great Broughton. This was Hannah Waugh, reputedly a witch with special powers. The witch told Polly that if her brother had been murdered, and the murderer was made to look upon the horseshoe, he would fall into a fit and convict himself. Hannah also made this curious prophecy: 'A'e thi daay; Bud lambs'll plaay, An' loup on t'grund wheer Anngrov' stands; Neea lahm sall ho'd it's steeans. Neea sod s'all hap up t'deead o' thi tweea han's.'

In simple terms, she forecast that the land upon which Anngrove Hall stood would become waste and barren; nothing would grow and lambs would gambol upon the site. Fortified by the old woman's prophecy, Polly intended to hang the horseshoe on the walls of the Black Swan at Stokesley, but until she had the opportunity of travelling there, she hung it on the walls of The Grange where she worked.

By sheer coincidence, her employer had arranged a card party, and among the guests was the master of Anngrove Hall. He happened to look upon the shoe, became sick and unsteady on his feet and asked to be driven home. As he was about to drive off, Polly shouted at him, 'Who murdered Edwards?'

Although the man denied any part in such a crime, the seeds of suspicion were sown, and his staff began to leave Anngrove Hall. One by one they left until the Hall closed and the Master was compelled to leave. He let the Hall, but the new tenant remained only for a very short time, as he could not obtain staff due to the reputation of the place. He was replaced by a relation of the former master, but the reputation remained; no one would work at Anngrove Hall.

And then, before this latest occupant departed, some men were digging for their ferrets in the stackyard at the Hall, when they came across several buttons from a coat. Excited, they dug further and eventually found a body with its skull battered in. But there is no account of the master of Anngrove Hall being brought to justice; perhaps he had died of natural causes, or perhaps there was a lack of evidence. We do not know, nor do we know the fate of his daughter.

After these macabre events, no one would live at the Hall. It fell into ruin and so the curious prophecy by Hannah Waugh was fulfilled.

But even today, no one is quite sure who killed Henry Edwards or, in fact, whether he was murdered. There is no proof that the found body was that of the missing man, but if it was not that of Henry Edwards, then who was it?

8 The Murder of a
Middlesbrough Taxi-Driver

The thriving industrial complex around Middlesbrough seems a world away from the rustic calm of the North York Moors, and yet part of Middlesbrough's southern suburbs, the area around Nunthorpe, is little more than a couple of miles from the edge of the National Park near Roseberry Topping. Today's boundaries, however, differ from those which existed prior to 1974. By that year, the huge industrial sprawl, collectively known as Teesside, had expanded to include Middlesbrough, Stockton, Thornaby, Billingham, Hartlepool, Guisborough and Redcar. In 1974, the area became the new County of Cleveland whose boundaries absorbed parts of Durham and some of the villages and market towns along the north-eastern extremities of the North Riding of Yorkshire.

Before 1974, Middlesbrough was part of the North Riding of Yorkshire, although it was a county borough in its own right, the only one within the North Riding. In the space of a few hectic years, Middlesbrough had grown from a small hamlet on the River Tees into a highly industrialized conglomoration of foundries, factories, docks, shops, streets and housing estates.

Some indication of the speed of its growth can be gauged by the fact that, even in 1825 when the world's first passenger-carrying railway line, the Stockton and

Darlington, was opened nearby, Middlesbrough was still a hamlet comprising only one farm. But there was the huge estuary of the Tees and lots of land nearby.

Even by 1829 the only house on the site was that farm; it had once been the site of a Benedictine chapel, but the originators of the railway line recognized the potential of the area for development as a port and a new town, chiefly for shipping coal. Five hundred acres were purchased and it was in that year that Middlesbrough's mammoth expansion started. Efforts were made to turn the River Tees into a series of docks, following which the Stockton and Darlington Railway was extended into Middlesbrough. By 1840 its first dock had been established and then in 1851, the discovery of iron ore in the nearby Cleveland Hills brought smelting plants to Middlesbrough. The iron and steel industry followed and this resulted in the phenomenal growth of the town and its satellite industries; by 1851, its population had grown to 7,631. In 1860, the tonnage of ocean-going ships on the River Tees was around 400,000 tons and by 1861, its population had grown to 19,416, an increase of almost 12,000 in ten years.

Prime Minister William Ewart Gladstone (1809-98) called Middlesbrough 'the youngest child of England's enterprise' and its iron/steel manufacturing capability earned it the name of 'the most remarkable seat of iron manufacture in Europe'. Some of the world's most famous bridges were built here including Sydney Harbour Bridge, the White Nile Bridge, the Menai Bridge, Lambeth Bridge, the Storstrom Bridge in Denmark, then the longest in Europe, Ghana's Volta River Bridge, the Tyne Bridge and Middlesbrough's own Transporter.

The area around Middlesbrough has never stopped expanding; the discovery of chemicals made it the home of ICI, there is ship-and oil-rig-building, a busy dockland and a massive range of other industries, both heavy and light. But the town is not all industry. There are some fine parks and gardens such as Stewart Park with its two lakes, aviary, animal enclosure and Captain Cook's Birthplace Museum. Albert Park has pleasant lawns and flower beds, and there are excellent museums and art galleries. Among Middlesbrough's noted buildings are the Town Hall, dating to 1899 with its magnificent panelled council chamber, and the Roman Catholic Cathedral, once a focus of interest, but now in a dangerous condition.

A new cathedral is under construction near the southern boundary, in the midst of a huge housing development at Coulby Newham. Close to Coulby Newham there is also Newham Grange Leisure Farm which offers a presentation of farming life, both old and new. This is based on a working farm with animals, machinery and farm services; it is open to the public during the summer months and provides a welcome hint of country life in this continually spreading modern town.

But almost overshadowed by the rows of houses and the busy shopping complex of Coulby Newham is the scene of an unsolved murder which has baffled the police since 1951. It was the year in which Fanny Blankers-Koen, the world's greatest woman runner, arrived at Middlesbrough to compete in the Middlesbrough and Cleveland Harriers Athletic Meeting.

Already the winner of four Olympic Gold Medals, she equalled her own 100 yards time of 10.8 seconds at Acklam Park that June, beating the British record by a tenth of a second. International soccer star, Wilf Mannion, was playing football for Middlesbrough's first division team and for England, but in the season which had ended that summer, he was injured. There was concern about his recovery, so he took a holiday at Staithes and made fine progress. During the same summer, an explosion at Eppleton Colliery near Easington, the second blast in the Durham coalfield within six weeks, killed seven miners and seriously injured another two. An intruder was caught climbing into a maid's bedroom at Buckingham Palace and John Thomas Straffen, aged twenty-one, was accused of murdering a child. The Conservatives won the October election after a brief spell of Labour Government and Winston Churchill became Prime Minister.

On Friday 16 November 1951, the England test cricketers were playing Pakistan at Lahore, while off Liverpool, the liner Empress of Scotland was heading into port for a civic reception. It was carrying home Princess Elizabeth and the Duke of Edinburgh after their royal visit to Canada and it was due to berth at Liverpool on the morning of Saturday 17 November 1951.

In Middlesbrough that same Friday evening, the 16th of November, a happy taxi driver called Edwin Youll was in a celebratory mood.

At forty-three years of age, he was a cheerful man who was always joking and he was highly popular with his workmates and friends. Known as Ted, he worked for Hornigold's Taxis at Middlesbrough, and had been employed there since August 1950. Among his work-mates, he was known as a real family man, one who was proud of his wife, Emma, his fine grown-up family and his comfortable home. This was in Bargate Street, North Ormesby, not far from the centre of Middlesbrough. Apart from his ability to laugh and joke, he was known as a quiet, peace-loving man who was very honest and genuine; he disliked getting involved in arguments and never mixed with persons of doubtful character. He was liked by everyone and was a man who could find a joke for every occasion; he could be the heart and soul of any party or any gathering of his workmates.

As this November weekend approached, little more than a month before Christmas, he was talking about plans for a cake he and his wife were arranging for their son's twenty-first birthday, and Edwin had also been informed he was to receive a special award from the Chief Constable. Some time earlier, he had been commended for assisting the police, but Edwin was to receive this award the following Tuesday 20 November 1951, for his work during the Middlesbrough Accident Prevention Council Courtesy Week scheme. It made him and his family very proud.

But Edwin Youll never celebrated his son's twenty-first birthday, nor did he received that award.

He was murdered. He was shot and savagely beaten about the head sometime between 6.25 p.m. and 6.35 p.m. that same Friday evening. Within the short space of about ten minutes, someone managed to kill Edwin Youll and flee the scene; in spite of intensive and prolonged enquiries, that person (or persons) has never been caught.

The early enquiries established his movements until 6.35 p.m. that Friday evening. In his taxi, he had collected two passengers, a man and a woman, from Middlesbrough railway station. That was at 6.05 p.m. Ten minutes later at 6.15 p.m., he deposited them in Marton Road, Middlesbrough.

Detailed enquiries later revealed that after this trip, Edwin had returned to Middlesbrough railway station, where, on the taxi rank at the Bridge Street side of the station, he had picked up two men. The time was between 6.20 p.m. and 6.25 p.m. He left by driving under Albert Bridge, and with the two men on board, signalled to a colleague that the Bridge Street rank at the station was clear. This was his last journey. At 6.35 p.m. his taxi was seen parked on Ladgate Lane, near the white gate at the entrance to the farm track which led to Newham Grange Farm. Ladgate Lane was a main thorough-fare. As the A1044, it led into town from nearby Yarm, and at the famous Blue Bell Inn, it became the A174. At that point, with the huge Blue Bell Inn overlooking the highway, it forked north into Middlesbrough Town Centre and east through Ormesby, Normanby and on towards Redcar.

The place where the body was found was very close to the border between jurisdiction of the North Riding Constabulary and Middlesbrough Police; the B1365 to Stokesley entered the A174 nearby, but, after some initial confusion, it was established that the body had been found within the area covered by Middlesbrough Police. The investigation was therefore the responsibility of that Force.

It was upon this busy main road, the A174, that Edwin's stationary taxi was spotted at 6.35 p.m. That road is now the B1380, because the modern A174 sweeps through the suburbs along its new route and the area around Newham Grange Farm is now a mass of houses. This area, once fields, is now called Coulby Newham.

It is almost certain that the murder was committed very near to 6.35 p.m. on Friday 16 November, and that many vehicles would be passing at the time, but no one has reported seeing anything suspicious. Three-quarters of an hour later, at 7.20 p.m. on this dark late-autumn evening, the body of Edwin Youll was found within sight of vehicles which passed along the main road. There is little doubt that darkness had concealed his body from passing traffic. He had apparently been dragged into the entrance to Newham Grange Farm, some fifteen yards from the main highway where there was a pool of blood.

Severe head injuries were evident and a trail of blood led from the main road to the position of the body. His taxi, registered number FUA 53, was not at that point. Someone had driven it back into the centre of Middlesbrough where, later that evening, it was found abandoned some four miles from where his body lay.

Led by the Chief Constable of Middlesbrough Police, Mr A.E. Edwards, an investigation was immediately launched. He was assisted by Superintendent G.S. MacDonald, Detective Chief Inspector B. Watson and Detective Sergeant M. Fairlamb. After preliminary examination of the scene, the body was removed for a post-mortem examination and immediate enquiries were launched in Middlesbrough, with particular emphasis upon tracing the man who had driven the taxi from Ladgate Lane to the point where it was abandoned in

Middlesbrough. He was described as 'of stiffish build, medium height, dressed in a lightish or fawn coloured mackintosh or overcoat with a belt, and a trilby hat.' The two sets of passengers collected separately by Edwin at the Railway Station were also wanted for questioning as house-to-house enquiries were established. Was the man described above one of those passengers?

Immediate assistance was sought from neighbouring police forces, particularly those which had ports, whether large or small, within their jurisdiction. Newcastle City police, Durham County and the North Riding Constabulary were all involved, while Middlesbrough's own detectives checked Middlesbrough's shipping lines. They sought members of any crew who might not have returned from shore leave or who might have returned in a blood-stained condition.

News of the murder hit the local papers the following day, Saturday 17 November; Middlesbrough's own paper, the *Evening Gazette*, carried an appeal for witnesses and announced that the police were anxious to trace two cars and a motor cycle which had been noticed on Ladgate Lane about 6.35 p.m., the time the taxi was seen parked. One car was a Ford and the other was a Standard, but the make of the motor-cycle was not known. That same Saturday, Middlesbrough's first division football team was playing Derby County and the Chief Constable, Mr Edwards, made an appeal to the crowd over the loudspeaker. He asked anyone to come forward if they had any information, however slight, about the movements of Edwin's taxi from 6 p.m. on Friday, or who might know the identity of the man whose description had been circulated, or especially the men collected by Edwin from the railway station. Had anyone been seen washing blood from themselves, or had anyone found a blood-stained weapon which might have been used?

That weekend was to provide an unpleasant shock for the investigating team, but it was also to provide more information about Edwin's two male passengers.

The shock came during the post-mortem examination because it revealed that Edwin Youll had been shot in the back of his head. The body had been moved from the scene before this discovery, a gross procedural error by the investigating team, but it was later established that the small bullet wound had not caused Edwin Youll's death.

The shot had come from a small calibre firearm, either a .22 or a .25. It was later established by ballistics experts that it was a .22 calibre weapon, probably a single-shot pistol or maybe a revolver. The Chief Constable announced that although this wound was in the back of Edwin's head, it had not caused his death. His death was due to a severe beating about the head and at the opening of the inquest, the pathologist, Dr Stanley Wray, said he had found the track of a bullet from the back of Mr Youll's neck; the bullet had travelled forwards and slightly downwards at an angle of about twenty degrees, but had not killed him.

Death was due to shock and haemorrhage associated with multiple fractures of the skull. There were cuts on the back of Mr Youll's head, an extensive compound fracture of the skull and damage to his brain. It had been a very severe attack. Bruises on his ankles suggested that Mr Youll had been dragged by the ankles, and among the tattoos on his body was one bearing his wife's name, Emma.

Furthermore, the absence of blood-stains in the taxi suggested that this attack had not occurred within the vehicle. It seemed Edwin had been shot in the taxi, the wound not generating a lot of blood, then he had been dragged into the road. Heavy bloodstains on the road surface suggested he had been violently attacked while lying in the road, following which he had been hauled some fifteen yards to where his body was quickly found.

It is incredible that this attack was never witnessed and that it occurred within such a short space of time; perhaps the stationary taxi, seen there at 6.35 p.m. shielded from passing traffic the swift and fatal assault on the defenceless Edwin Youll? It is also surprising that so few people recalled seeing the taxi parked at this busy point, although it must be remembered that it was a dark November evening. During the actual killing, the vehicle may have been parked in darkness.

The belated discovery that a firearm was involved then caused the police to make late, but detailed searches of the ground and undergrowth in the vicinity of Ladgate Lane and around the streets where the taxi had been located. They sought a discarded firearm or some spent ammunition, but although mine detectors were employed to sweep the undergrowth near the farm entrance, nothing was found.

Another item that was sought was the weapon which had caused such horrific injuries to Edwin Youll. No indication of what it might have been was published during the early days of the investigation, although the police did announce they were seeking something like a small hatchet or axe, or even a heavy tyre lever. They ascertained that no tools from the taxi had been used during the attack, nor were any missing.

The motive for the murder remained a mystery too, because robbery appeared not to be the reason as £4 cash was found on Edwin's body.

It is possible, of course, that robbery was the motive and that the killers had been disturbed during their attack. No other motive presented itself because detailed enquiries into Edwin Youll's private life showed that he was a very honest man who lived a good life. The police established that no one appeared to bear any malice towards him. But enquiries during the weekend did produce more information about the two suspects. It was confirmed that one was between 5' 8'' to 5' 10'' tall, well built, wearing a fawn or light coloured mackintosh, raincoat or overcoat with a belt at the back. He was dark-haired, although he might have been wearing a dark-coloured trilby hat. It was felt that one of the witnesses might have confused his dark hair with a hat. This description roughly corresponded to that of the man already being sought, that is the man who had abandoned the taxi in Marsh Road, near Middlesbrough town centre.

The second man was shorter than the other; he wore a dark-coloured suit but no hat. He might have carried his hat, however, as he and his colleague entered Edwin's taxi at the station around 6.20 p.m.

The lack of positive progress and the lack of information coming from the public prompted Middlesbrough Police Authority to offer a reward of £500 for information leading to the arrest of the murderer or murderers of Edwin Youll. But that reward has never been claimed, although it may have produced some results.

On the Sunday night following the murder, and no doubt prompted by the publicity, a peculiar note was found by a cleaner in the buffet at Waterloo Station, London. She discovered the note at 11 p.m. and the text was as follows:

Saki and me got clean away from that job. The driver has had it now. I held him down and Saki kicked the back of his head in. We dragged him into a hedge back and then drove the taxi to Middlesbro. It sure was a good idea doing the job near the Blue Bell because ...

At that point, the paper had been torn and the rest was missing. It seems that the cleaner had found it, discussed it with a colleague and then taken it home to show her husband. He had read about the Middlesbrough murder and so they had handed the note to the police.

So was this a genuine note or was it a hoax? Of some significance was the fact that, at the time of its discovery in London on the Sunday night, there had been no publicity about the fact that two men might be involved and, so far as the police were aware, no mention of the proximity of the Blue Bell Hotel. Furthermore, the claims that the back of Mr Youll's head had been kicked could also be true, although, significantly, the note did not mention the shooting. Perhaps, if this was from the killers, they did not appreciate the skills of a pathologist in being able to determine this fact?

Later, the Chief Constable did announce that heavy boots could have caused the injuries to the back of Edwin Youll's head.

From the note, three other points emerged. The name Saki could refer to someone of continental origin, it may have come from the name of the cup-bearer in the *Rubáiyát of Omar Khayám*, or it could even have been copied from the novelist Hector Hugh Monro (1870-1916) who used the pseudonym of Saki. It is also the name of a Japanese drink. In addition, it is used to describe hawkers and tinkers in the North of England. In the North Riding, this name was probably spelt Sackie or even Sacky and I remember many such persons who bore this nickname. They travelled from door to door, sometimes on foot and sometimes with a horse and cart, dealing in rags, scrap metal and other waste odds-and-ends.

The second point to emerge from the letter is the term 'hedge back'; this is a local term for the bottom of a hedge – I do not think it is a widespread term, other districts using different terms, such as hedgerows or hedge bottoms. But in North Yorkshire, we still call them 'hedge backs' which does suggest to me that the note was written by a local person.

The third point also suggests the note was written by a local person because of the abbreviated form of spelling Middlesbrough. Middlesbro' remains a very popular method of shortening the name of this town and is widely used in the north-east.

The discovery of this note, which contained facts not known to the general public such as the kicking on the back of the head, prompted a good response from the public who submitted names of persons called Sacky, Saki or Sackie. It also caused many men bearing this name to come forward for elimination. But the clearly legible handwriting, in ball-point pen upon notepaper from an ordinary notepad, was never identified and no useful information was forthcoming because of it. The general feeling was that the writer knew a lot about Middlesbrough and the surrounding area, while the term 'It sure was' suggested it was the work of a young person who was then emulating the behaviour and speech used in American films, then very popular with young people.

The murder, and the fear it generated in and around Middlesbrough, did result in some terror among the public and among taxi-drivers in particular. Rumours of other serious crimes circulated – one said a woman had been found with her throat cut, and another claimed a woman had been strangled in the town.

Nurses and other late workers were afraid to travel home alone, and a ship at Hull was boarded and searched by detectives who felt the killer(s) might be escaping upon it. But all these stories were without foundation. Two similar crimes in other parts of the country were also investigated. One involved the murder of a Birmingham taxi-driver three years earlier. In this case, the driver was found shot dead in the driving seat of his taxi at Burton-on-Trent.

The killer, who was never found, was believed to be a member of the Royal Air Force as, two days later, a service revolver and some RAF papers were discovered in a field half a mile away from the scene of this crime. Another similar crime occurred in Kent when someone attempted to murder a taxi-driver by stabbing him. This happened only seven days before the Middlesbrough murder, but the driver survived the attack.

The files on both these cases were sent to Middlesbrough CID for comparisons to be made, but no known link was established.

On Tuesday 20 November 1951, as the investigation continued, Mrs Emma Youll had a proud, but emotional duty to perform. She had to receive the special award won by her late husband during the Middlesbrough Accident Prevention Council Courtesy Week for his actions in going to the assistance of a blind man who was struggling to cross the road in heavy traffic. Edwin Youll's action was described as a most courteous and humane act, typical of his general demeanour.

During this period, there is little doubt that the 'Saki' note did produce a wealth of very useful publicity and it helped to create a deeper public interest in the crime. Floods of information came in from the general public and from other police forces and so great was the response that additional office space had to be utilized at Middlesbrough Police Headquarters.

At one stage, more than fifty letters a day were arriving as more detectives were drafted onto the investigation and the momentum increased. In addition, the reward was increased to £1,000.

Then an elderly gentleman recalled thinking he had seen the two suspects on the No.73 United bus which had left Middlesbrough at 9.45 p.m. on the day of the murder *en route* to Saltburn. The bus left Stockton at 9.18 p.m. and travelled via Middlesbrough during its trip to Saltburn. The passenger remembered seeing two men sitting in the fourth seat from the front on the lower deck. In his opinion, they were behaving rather strangely and one of them was carrying a fawn raincoat. They remained on the bus until it reached Grangetown, but might have then got off at either Redcar or Saltburn.

It seems that a crime was committed on that bus during that journey too, when £8 in fares was stolen from the conductress's cupboard. This was in the panelling at the foot of the stairs leading to the upper deck. The money disappeared between Dormanstown and Redcar. The police placed some importance upon this sighting, especially upon the evidence of a Redcar insurance agent who overheard the conversation between the two suspects while on this bus.

Another witness who later came forward was a cyclist. He felt sure he had seen the victim's taxi being driven into Middlesbrough half-an-hour after the murder. He claimed it had to pull up behind him when he stopped at a crossing.

He said he was startled at the speed of the taxi which approached him from behind at 7.10 p.m. on the day of Edwin's death, the Friday evening. At the time, he was in Longford Street, between Ayresome Street and Parliament Road.

He was sure this was the taxi in question because he recalled seeing FUA and the figure 5 on the registration plate, and he was also able to supply a more detailed description of the two suspects who were in the taxi. One had fair hair and was wearing an American-style Stetson trilby with a wide brim, and he had a light raincoat. This description is similar to the man who drove the taxi to Marsh Road after the murder, the colour of his hair differing slightly. Such variations in a witness's observations are not unusual and can vary with light or even faulty vision.

With him was a dark man who was driving the taxi when it was seen by the cyclist. He was wearing a dark or blue suit and wore no hat. He was said to be carrying a satin-lined raincoat on his arm, a curious act – unless it was concealing a blood-stained item of his own clothing?

The taxi continued along Union Street at a high speed when it turned down either Glebe Road or Pauls Road and this evidence enabled the police to completely account for the movements of the taxi that Friday evening from 6 p.m. until its discovery, and to be more positive about their suspects.

But in spite of continuing enquiries and intense investigation by Middlesbrough Police, no one was arrested for this crime. The identity of the killer(s) and their motive in murdering Edwin Youll, the happy taxi-driver, have never been determined.

There were mistakes by the police, the most telling of which was the removal of Mr Youll's body before a proper investigation had been made at the scene. But their determination to track down the murderer(s) did pinpoint every move of his taxi from 6.05 p.m., the time he collected two innocent passengers from Middlesbrough Station, through to the time he picked up the two suspects only twenty minutes later, until it was found abandoned after his death.

A picture of the two suspects, albeit very sketchy, does emerge, and here it must be borne in mind that all these sightings would be during the hours of darkness on an autumn night in conditions that were far from ideal. This would lead to variations in the witnesses' descriptions and it was perhaps that darkness that shielded the killers as they committed their crime in Ladgate Lane?

Cleveland's new Police Headquarters stands only a few yards from the place where Edwin's body was found and when I asked if there had been any developments in this 1951 case, enquiries were made on my behalf, but the answer was in the negative.

The murder of Edwin Youll remains a mystery, but the file will never be closed.

9 Murder at Marske-by-the-Sea

Marske-by-the-Sea stands literally between the heather and the sea and is popular with both holidaymakers and residents. Although it is now a highly attractive commuter village for Teesside, its houses and other buildings reveal a more ancient history. Marske Hall, for example, with its facade of three domed towers, dates to 1625 and it is now a Cheshire Home. The Church of St Mark, which stands dramatically on the very brink of the cliffs to act as a landmark for sailors, contains a fine thirteenth-century wayside cross and a Norman font which is adorned with rich carvings. This nineteenth-century building occupies the site of the former church of St Germain which was demolished in 1820, while within the graveyard lies the father of the great Yorkshire explorer, Captain James Cook. A local legend surrounding this old man says he lived until he was seventy without ever learning a single letter of the alphabet, whereupon he then taught himself to read so that he could follow the exploits and voyages of his world-famous son.

The centre of Marske contains some delightful stone cottages and houses while those close to the coast overlook the brooding greyness of the North Sea. A splendid beach of yellow sand stretches north-east towards Redcar and between these neighbouring communities, there is a long expanse of open grassland and beach which is bordered by the coast road. Inland from the sea, Marske has expanded into a conglomoration of new housing estates and schools.

This new urban sprawl has taken Marske's boundaries very close to those of Redcar, so much so that in some cases the distinction between the two places is not easily seen.

Like Marske, Redcar was once a fishing village. It has now grown into a busy and interesting seaside resort with a truly magnificent beach of very firm yellow sands, a fine promenade, popular race-course, good shopping and excellent leisure facilities which are popular with the people of Teesside. Like Marske, it has expanded so that it now merges with industrial Teesside along with surrounding villages and towns such as Coatham and Dormanstown. Even so, fishermen still operate from Redcar beach, resting their boats high on the sands while they're not at sea. Redcar's strong links with the sea are evident in the Zetland Lifeboat Museum on the seafront which contains the oldest lifeboat in the world.

Redcar's wide main street contains very few old houses, although the church is interesting for its reredos which has fine traceried panels depicting six north-east saints – Cuthbert, Hilda, Wilfred, Aiden, Oswald and Columba. One famous resident of Redcar was the traveller, scholar and writer, Gertrude Bell (1868-1926) who lived at Red Barnes House. Described as one of the most astonishing women of her time, she journeyed widely in the Near East and contributed to the founding of modern Iraq.

Side by side on this bracing north-east coast, the townships of Redcar and Marske were once part of the North Riding of Yorkshire; today, they are in County Cleveland having been transferred into this new administrative county in 1974. Between them is a railway line which runs inland from Redcar station, passing through suburban streets on its route to Marske; as it nears Marske, this line forms a positive dividing line between the two communities, and stretching alongside this line as it enters Marske, is Redcar's Green Lane.

At the time of writing, this remains a green track between the fields and I walked along it shortly before compiling these notes. It starts near the coast road at Redcar with the truly rural stretch beginning close to the Redcar Rugby Union Football Club's MacKinley Park entrance. There this narrow, leafy lane is barely wide enough to accommodate a car, although it is just possible to drive a small vehicle along its unmade surface towards Marske.

As it nears Marske, Green Lane runs alongside the railway towards the stone-built bridge which spans the line. The road in question leads from Marske's village-centre roundabout towards the southern edge of Redcar, emerging at one of the two new roundabouts not far from the racecourse. Once this road was the A174, but due to the changes in recent years, it is now a quiet minor road having been superceded by the amended route of the A174. As this runs from Middlesbrough into Saltburn, it now bypasses Marske.

But as one approaches the railway bridge when travelling from Marske, the end of the green lane lies below the road level to the right, almost adjacent to the bridge. It is a delightful lane, one which is frequented by Sunday afternoon strollers and by lovers during the evenings.

It was here, at the Marske end of Green Lane, that the body of an attractive young woman was found in the autumn of 1963. She had died from asphyxiation and her killer has never been traced.

Mrs Linda Margaret Cook, who was twenty-two years old, had lived with her husband, Michael, in a flat in Kirkleatham Lane, Redcar. It was above the doctor's surgery where she worked as a receptionist. She and Michael had been married for two years and he worked as an insurance agent in the area, but the couple had decided to separate. Michael Cook went to live in lodgings at Queen Street, Redcar, while Linda moved into a flat at No.

7 Newcomen Terrace, Redcar. She moved into that flat on Friday 20 September 1963.

Two days later, on Sunday 22 September, she was found dead in Green Lane.

Detective Superintendent Albert Websdale and Detective Inspector Arthur Taylor of the North Riding Constabulary were put in charge of the murder investigation and immediately visited the scene. Two facts were rapidly established – Mrs Cook had not been subjected to any sexual assault, and the absence of signs of a struggle at the scene suggested she had been murdered elsewhere.

It seemed that someone had brought her body to this quiet place where it was found at 7 a.m. on the Sunday morning by the driver of a milk lorry. Her body was lying about one hundred yards from the then A174; it was on the verge of Green Lane a yard or two from the railway boundary fence and not far from a platelayer's cabin.

The lorry-driver who found Linda told how he had made his discovery. The body was lying by the roadside and he got the impression it had been placed there after death because the long grass surrounding it was undisturbed. Her clothes were neatly arranged too, suggesting the killer had placed the body in what seemed to be a sleeping position. Had the murder occurred there, or had there been a struggle at the scene, any disturbances to the grass would have revealed this.

As the body was removed for a post-mortem, which was to establish asphyxiation as the cause of death, the investigating team set about interviewing everyone who knew the vivacious redhead. It was quickly established that she had left a local hotel at 2.30 p.m. on Saturday afternoon, and it was possible she had called at a local corner shop soon afterwards to buy some corned beef. There the trail ended.

The police were anxious to trace her movements and her contacts from that time until her body was found, i.e.

from 2.30 p.m. on Saturday 21 September until 7 a.m. on Sunday 22 September, a matter of sixteen-and-a-half hours.

An appeal was launched in the local press during which Detective Superintendent Websdale asked to come forward anyone who might have seen Linda after 2.30 p.m. that Saturday afternoon until sometime late on Saturday night or even into the early hours of Sunday morning. She might have been visiting friends at their home, might have gone to a dance, a club or a party, or been socializing at a local inn. But very little information was forthcoming.

The problem of filling in these 'lost' hours, coupled with the possibility that she had been killed elsewhere and dumped in Green Lane, presented some difficulties to the investigators. There was a lack of clues and evidence, consequently the nature of this enquiry was such that it was decided by the Chief Constable of the North Riding, Mr J.R. Archer-Burton, that the more experienced skills and expertise of Scotland Yard was required. Two detectives from the Yard's Murder Squad were therefore called in; this was an unusual step and is probably the last time the Yard was called in to assist this provincial police force.

The officers were Detective Chief Superintendent William Tennent and Detective Sergeant Raymond Peling, Tennant having been the man in charge of the investigation into the theft of Goya's painting, 'The Duke of Wellington'.

After travelling north late on Monday night, they began their work on Tuesday 24 September by renewing appeals for witnesses who might be able to fill in those 'lost' hours.

All the public houses and clubs in Redcar, Marske and district were visited and photographs of Linda were shown to the customers, but little information was forthcoming. Anyone travelling between Redcar and Marske along the line by train during the material times was asked to reflect upon anything suspicious or odd that they might have seen near Marske bridge. Courting couples who used Green Lane were asked to come forward if they had been in the vicinity on Saturday night or Sunday morning, particularly if they had noticed anyone of Linda's description or a suspicious vehicle.

One of those who did come forward was Michael Cook who explained that he and Linda had separated the previous Friday and had decided to live apart. He provided the police with the background of Linda's life as he knew it, and gave them every possible assistance. He was swiftly eliminated from the enquiries.

But the efforts of the police were narrowing the span of those 'lost' hours. By Wednesday, a witness came forward to say that Linda had been seen shopping at 4.30 p.m. on Saturday afternoon. She was then wearing the clothes in which she had been dressed when leaving the hotel at 2.30 p.m., a brown sheepskin jacket and blue jeans. Whilst engaged upon that shopping trip, she had carried her sheepskin jacket and had purchased some groceries. These were later found at her new flat, thus indicating she had returned there.

When her body was found, she was wearing a pink woollen two-piece suit with a tight fitting or pencil-slim skirt, and black leather court shoes with stiletto heels.

Corresponding to this narrowing of the 'lost' hours, more people came forward to say they had been in Green Lane during the material hours, but none produced anything of value to the enquiry. Simultaneously, more and more of Linda's friends and contacts were being traced and interviewed, thus narrowing the investigation. Sadly, none of these contacts could produce any information which was of genuine value.

Detective Chief Superintendent Tennent did express the opinion that Linda had known her killer, and he appeared on local television to appeal for more of her contacts and friends to come forward. The gap of 'lost' hours, reduced but slightly, did remain, and a renewed campaign was introduced to produce witnesses. Bus conductors, railway employees, taxi drivers and others in public service were revisited and interviewed, and the local pubs, clubs and places of public resort were again visited and photographs of Linda shown.

Another avenue of investigation opened with the realization that the street fair which followed Stokesley Show had taken place on the Saturday night of her death. This attraction was a magnet for young people from a great distance, consequently intense enquiries were launched to see whether Linda had visited Stokesley that Saturday.

Stokesley is a charming North Yorkshire market town some twelve miles from Redcar. Its annual agricultural show is the largest in the region, attracting more than 20,000 visitors, but like many events of this kind, there is more to attract youngsters than the livestock and agricultural exhibits and displays. Sideshows, music, bars and the whole panoply of entertainment are here during the show. At the time of Linda's death, Stokesley Show was always held on the third Thursday in September, but since 1968 it has moved to the Saturday following the third Thursday.

One massive additional attraction is Stokesley Fair; since 1859, this has been an annual event which runs in conjunction with the Show and it draws huge crowds. The Fair alone is a four-day event which begins on the Wednesday before the Show and continues until late on the Saturday night. Its array of big rides, stalls, funfairs and caravans fills the entire length of the town's wide main street and adjoining market-place. Some seventy showmen attend and the normal shops in the town close down during that time.

It was an immense task to determine whether Linda, either alone or with one or more companions, had visited Stokesley on the Saturday night before her death was discovered. Although the Fair had departed, detailed enquiries were made at Stokesley and from those fairground personnel who had moved on; some had moved to a new site at North Ormesby near Middlesbrough where another fair had opened. But this new line of enquiry produced nothing.

Another line of enquiry which was not publicized during the early days of the investigation involved Linda's detailed diary. She kept a daily account of her activities and it included the names and places where she met friends, both men and women, and many of these meetings were recorded only by the Christian names of those she met. The police sifted through this diary with care, gradually tracing those who were featured within its pages, but like other facets of this enquiry, it also produced nothing of real substance. The blue-covered diary was in her handbag which was beside her body when it was found. I find this somewhat strange – if the killer had for one moment thought he was mentioned in her diary, he would surely have discarded it. It is also odd that he left the handbag with her body – that act implies a very cool killer if he could think of bringing the bag from where ever he had killed her and carefully placing it beside her body. Why did he undertake this little act at the scene where time would be desperately short?

A week later, on the Saturday following her death, a policewoman was dressed in clothes similar to the ones worn by Linda during her Saturday afternoon shopping trip. I cannot establish whether this lady followed Linda's known progress around Redcar on the previous Saturday afternoon in those clothes, but posed photographs did appear in the local papers and on television in the hope that this would jog the memory of any possible witnesses.

This appeared to have some effect because on the following day, Sunday, a witness came forward to say that a woman answering Linda's description had travelled on the last-but-one bus on Saturday 21 September as it motored upon the Dormanstown-Green Lane Estate route. This was the No. 71 United bus which left The Fleet, Dormanstown at 10.10 p.m. that Saturday and arrived at the junction of Laburnum Road and Canterbury Road, Redcar, at 10.25 p.m. The No. 71 bus stop at the junction of Laburnum Road and Canterbury Road was just under half-a-mile from the Redcar end of Green Lane, and only two stops away from the Lane itself. The lady who corresponded to Linda's description got off the bus at the Laburnum Road/Canterbury Road junction and she was alone at the time.

The police regarded this as important new evidence and asked for more persons who had used that bus to come forward in an attempt to confirm this sighting. Later, others did come forward and the police managed to trace several further passengers, but the sighting was never substantiated. Had this been so, it would have shortened those 'lost' hours still further; the police did say, however, that no portion of a bus ticket was found in Linda's handbag, consequently there was no proof she had ridden on that bus.

Another theory which was expounded was that Linda had met her death in a motor-car, something very feasible bearing in mind the place and nature of the dumping of her body.

In this instance it was suggested the car might have been stolen. A search of the lists of crimes reported in the area that weekend revealed that no cars had been reported stolen, although the police knew that many drivers left keys in the ignition switches and their car doors unlocked. So had the killer 'borrowed' a car for this meeting with Linda, killed her within it, and then returned it during the night hours so that the owner had never known it had been moved?

Occasionally, a motorist would only know that his or her car had been unlawfully used because of its additional mileage, a shortage of petrol or its changed parking position. Sometimes, damage occurred on these illicit trips, or items such as beer bottles, sweets and other odds and ends were left in the cars, thus revealing their secret use. If a car was returned undamaged, the owner seldom made a formal report to the police; only if it vanished from sight did he report such 'taking of a motor vehicle without the owner's consent'.

The police therefore launched an appeal for motorists to examine their cars to see if this had occurred, and asked for those who had noticed something odd about their vehicles last weekend, to come forward. Stress was placed on this appeal by suggesting a borrowed car could have been used by the killer of Linda Cook as a means of transporting her body to Green Lane. But, like all the earlier appeals, this one produced nothing.

It became evident to the police that someone, or perhaps several persons, were withholding vital information because the case had attracted widespread publicity but had revealed so little information. Apart from a possible sighting on a late Saturday night bus, the 'lost' hours in Linda's life remained a puzzle.

How was it that a young woman with so many friends and contacts, who was so well known both because of her work at the doctor's surgery and in her private life, could avoid being seen in Redcar by someone who knew her? And where did she spend that Saturday night? And with whom did she spend the evening?

Following widespread appeals in the local pubs, clubs, dance halls, cinemas and other public places, including the football match between Middlesbrough and Bradford at Middlesbrough's Ayresome Park, and after publicity in the papers, on radio and on television, some three hundred people did come forward with snippets of information. The police were very grateful for this response, but Chief Superintendent Tennent of the Yard did express a feeling that among certain individuals there was determined reluctance to help.

'It has come to my notice,' he said. 'That one or two people have been heard to boast that they know something, but they do not wish to become involved.'

Enquiries spread into the nearby moorland and hills to the village of Castleton where Linda had once lived, but no one there could help.

Chief Superintendent Tennent appealed to the public to consider how they would react if their own wife/sister/daughter/sweetheart/friend has been the victim. But these efforts produced nothing.

As the investigation lengthened into October, it became clear that no new information was forthcoming. Every possible avenue of enquiry had been explored and exhausted but the teams of some twenty detectives continued to check and recheck the information already gleaned. They continued with house-to-house enquiries, showing Linda's photograph around Redcar but the investigation gradually ground to a halt. There were no fresh leads to explore.

The police were left with the feeling that someone in Redcar or Marske was concealing the killer, perhaps unknowingly, and the Scotland Yard team returned to London leaving this Yorkshire crime unsolved.

When I checked the current situation with Cleveland Police, I was told that no new leads had been established, but that the file remains open.

There is still time for the killer of Linda Cook to be brought to justice.

10   The Man-hunt of
Malton and Dalby Forest

Dalby Forest covers a huge tract of high ground to the north-east of Pickering, one of North Yorkshire's delightful market-towns. The forest comprises a mature and dense covering of conifers and is a direct result of the Forestry Commission's afforestation plans for the North York Moors. The planting of these massive numbers of trees began in 1920 when it was realized that the impoverished soil and inhospitable conditions of the wild upland regions could economically produce conifers, if nothing else! The trees were therefore planted as a crop and are now a valuable part of the nation's economy.

Dalby Forest, which is just one of several forests in this area, covers a spectacular range of hills and dales, and the dense woodland is criss-crossed with a highly complex network of rough tracks. It is rich with wildlife too and it was the developing forest which soon became recognized as a very valuable recreational resource.

Visitors were encouraged to explore the area, a forest drive was introduced and this was complemented by forest trails, picnic sites, viewpoints and an information centre. There is a Forest Visitor Centre in the village of Low Dalby and nearby are other facilities such as a camping and caravan park and cabin accommodation for holidays. It is a fascinating area and deep among the scented trees there is, at times, an uncanny silence broken occasionally by the call of the jay or sounds of a startled deer.

Access to the western end of the forest drive, for which there is a small toll, is via the village of Low Dalby which is north of Thornton-le-Dale, while entry from the east is through Bickley and Langdale End near Hackness which is not far from Scarborough and the coast. In the winter months, Dalby Forest is utterly at peace and almost deserted but during the summer months, the area is especially busy with tourists and holidaymakers.

But it was during the summer of 1982, that the tranquillity of Dalby Forest was shattered when it became the focal point of England's largest manhunt. Huge numbers of armed police hunted a man who had shot and killed two North Yorkshire policemen and a gentleman from Nottinghamshire, in addition to shooting at and injuring a third policeman. It was a tense, frightening and harrowing time, not only for the police officers engaged on the hunt, but also for the residents of the forest communities, the people in the surrounding market-towns and villages, and the public in general.

The case left in its wake several minor mysteries.

As a police inspector, I was involved in this hunt from the outset, my role being that of the Press Liaison Officer for the North Yorkshire Police. My task was to establish and maintain a working relationship with radio, television and newspapers and to liaise with those in charge of the investigation so that the public, both in the UK and overseas, was kept fully informed and advised at all stages.

As news of the first murder was made known, none of us could have guessed that such a horrifying drama was to unfold and that hundreds of officers throughout the country would be engaged non-stop upon a desperate search and highly demanding investigation which would endure for the next eighteen days. In the absence of Detective Chief Superintendent Strickland Carter, the head of North Yorkshire CID, who was overseas, the investigation became the responsibility of his deputy, Detective Superintendent John Carlton.

The first murder was committed near Harrogate on Thursday 17 June 1982 when twenty-nine-year-old PC David Haigh was shot dead during a routine patrol. In his white Ford Fiesta panda car, he had left Harrogate Police Station at 7.30 a.m., taking with him some summonses which he was to serve during his rounds. Two hours later, when he failed to respond to a radio call, his colleagues began a search and shortly before 10 a.m. discovered his body in a parking area beside the B6451 Otley-Blubberhouses Road. The location was the well-known Warren Point beauty spot and picnic site at Norwood Edge, part of the ancient Forest of Knaresborough. His car was parked with the driver's door open and PC Haigh was lying beside it. He had died from a head wound inflicted at point-blank range by a small calibre gun, probably a .22 pistol. Lying under his body was a clipboard upon which he had written 'Clive Jones, born 18.10.44, Leeds. n.f.a.' and the car registration number KYG 326P.

It seemed that he had left his own car to interrogate a suspicious person in another vehicle at this spot; the suspect had given a false name and a date of birth, and PC Haigh had managed to write down the car number before he was shot. 'Leeds' indicated the place of birth and the letters n.f.a. mean 'no fixed address.'

The killer and his car had vanished. A detailed search of the area and the verges of the roads leading away from the picnic site, failed to trace the weapon and so it became evident that the killer had not discarded the gun. We knew that an armed murderer was now being hunted. A computer check of the car number revealed that it belonged to a green Citröen GSX2 1975 model and later enquiries revealed that it had been bought in London from a car dealer on 13 January by a man called R.D. Carlisle. The dealer remembered this sale; Carlisle paid £475 for the car and he handed over the cash at a London Tube Station. He was described as between thirty and thirty-five, clean-shaven and well dressed. He had a holdall full of money, spoke with a northern accent and said he had just come off an oil-rig and was returning to the north.

Following the murder, a young man was swiftly arrested; he had been living rough in the nearby woods, he was armed and had been amusing himself by taking pot shots at birds and animals. Furthermore, he was named in one of the summonses due to be served by PC Haigh. But his rifle was an air weapon, so this was not the killer; after intense questioning, he was soon released, a most relieved man.

This meant that the killer was at large in the green Citroën and so presented an enormous danger to any police officer who attempted to stop and interrogate him. Such warnings were issued as the registration number was circulated to police officers throughout the UK and to the public by courtesy of the press, radio and television. One striking feat of observation was recorded at this stage.

A seventeen-year-old youth on a motor-cycle passed the Warren picnic site every weekday on his way to work; on the day of the murder, as with every morning, he stopped there for a few minutes rest on his long journey. This was just after half-past seven and he saw the green Citroën. It was parked and a man was asleep in the driving seat.

He described that man as being in his thirties with dark curly hair and tanned or swarthy features with a bulbous nose. He had been wearing a light coloured canvas anorak with a hood, but no more could be seen due to his position in the car. Furthermore, the lad remembered the car number and so we had proof that the car had been parked there prior to PC Haigh's arrival, and we had a brief description of the suspect. His recollection of the car number and description of the man was remarkable – and highly valuable.

That first weekend also produced more good news. A

farmer at Ledsham near Garforth in West Yorkshire, which is just off the A1 near Selby Fork, had decided to take his family out for a meal on Sunday evening.

However, the appalling June weather, with rain, winds and mist, caused him to worry about his ripening wheat crop. He decided to inspect it before leaving home and as he entered his field, he noticed car tracks leading into the centre. He discovered that a car had been driven seven hundred yards into the middle of the field where it had been abandoned after being concealed from the road by a natural hillock. It was a very clever hiding place among waist-high wheat, and it may not have been found for many weeks. It was the green Citroën KYF 326P. The car was removed to the Forensic Science Laboratory at Wetherby where it was subjected to intense scientific examination. But where was the armed driver?

By the Wednesday which marked the end of the first week of enquiries, the killer had not been caught and we arranged to stage a reconstruction of the events at Norwood Edge. It would take place on the morning of Thursday 24 June, exactly one week after the murder. Three panda cars were to follow the three routes from Harrogate to the picnic site, any one of which could have been traversed by PC Haigh on the morning of his death. All vehicles passing the scene between 6 a.m. and 9.30 a.m. would be stopped, and the drivers and passengers would be asked if they could recall noticing anything on Warren picnic site or the approach roads the previous Thursday morning. In particular, the police were anxious to learn whether anyone had seen either the white police car or the hurried departure of the green Citroën.

But before this reconstruction was actually implemented, news of another killing reached Detective Superintendent Carlton and his officers in the Harrogate Incident Room. They learned from Nottinghamshire Police that on Tuesday 22 June, Mr George Luckett, a fifty-two-year-old electrician who lived at the village of Girton near Lincoln, had been shot dead. His wife, Sylvia, had also been shot in the head, but she managed to drag herself a hundred yards to a neighbour's house where she raised the alarm. Although she had a bullet in her head, she survived that awful ordeal.

It seemed that the couple had disturbed a man who was trying to steal their car; this was a brown Rover 2.6 litre saloon and its registration number was VAU 875S. That car was missing. The cause of Mr Luckett's death was a shot from a .22 weapon, probably a pistol. In the early stages of this enquiry, there was little cause even to consider that this murder was linked to that of PC Haigh, although it did become evident that the Girton murder may be linked to an attack the previous day upon a seventy-five-old Mrs Freda Jackson at Blyton Carr near Gainsborough in Lincolnshire. On Sunday 20 June, she had been bound and gagged, then robbed of a mere £4.50 and some food. She felt her attacker was more interested in the food than the small sum of money.

By chance, a gamekeeper had been patrolling the nearby private woods some nine days prior to the attack of 20 June and he had noticed a man living rough; beside the shelter he had constructed, there was a green Citroën car.

This was six days before PC Haigh's death, but the gamekeeper had noted that its number was KYF 326P. The gamekeeper told the man to leave the grounds because it was private land, and the man obeyed. Upon learning of the North Yorkshire manhunt, the gamekeeper passed this information to the local police and in this way it was established that these crimes could be connected. The gamekeeper described that man as being in his early thirties, about 5' 8'' to 5' 10'' tall, slim with dark, curly hair. At that time he was wearing jeans, tan shoes, a fawn raincoat, brown cotton gloves and a gold-coloured bracelet, a description which matched that given by Mrs Jackson.

Was it possible that the driver of that car had, after 11

June, driven up to Harrogate where he had shot PC Haigh (17 June), then driven back down to Ledsham where he had abandoned the Citroën (17 June), then somehow found his way further south to Blyton Carr near Gainsborough where he robbed a lady of £4.50 and some food, then continued to Girton where he had killed Mr Luckett on 22 June? As these suspicions formed in the minds of the investigating police officers, the bullet which killed PC Haigh was ballistically examined and compared with that which had killed Mr Luckett.

They had come from the same gun, a fact which elevated the investigation into one of grave national concern.

By Wednesday 24 June, therefore, it was known that a very dangerous man was at large somewhere in England in the Luckett's stolen brown 2.6 litre Rover.

He was armed and willing to use his gun at the slightest provocation. Through the news media, the public was warned not to approach the stolen Rover or the man who was driving it, but to report any sightings to the police without delay. Police officers were also warned to use extreme caution when approaching any vehicle parked in an isolated position and containing a lone male occupant. So who was the killer and where was he heading next?

It seemed inconceivable that he would return to North Yorkshire and so every police force in the country was warned that he might strike again, this time within their area. All air- and sea-ports were watched, customs points checked especially where they functioned near oil-rigs while all ferries and British Rail stations were scrutinized. It was now a major national manhunt which resulted in headline stories in the newspapers, on radio and television.

Meanwhile, behind the scenes, some fine police work was being undertaken and the name of a possible suspect had emerged. For legal reasons, this name could not be released to the public because widespread publicity of a suspect could be seen as likely to prejudice a fair trial should he ever be brought to justice. A defence lawyer could claim that no jury, having witnessed the widespread media coverage, could give the accused a fair hearing. Besides, at this stage, the name being considered was nothing more than a suspect. More evidence was needed before the police could be positive that he was the man they sought.

Our prime suspect came to notice because a police officer in the Summonses and Warrants Department of West Yorkshire Police at Wakefield was sifting through some arrest warrants which had not been executed. One of them was for a man called Barry Peter Prudom, alias Barry Peter Edwards. He was wanted on warrant for failing to answer to his bail on a charge of severely wounding a Leeds motorist with an iron bar. When Prudom's particulars were examined, it was discovered he had been born in Leeds on 18.10.1944. Knowing that it is easy to give a false name at a moment's notice, but more difficult to give a false date of birth, this name was passed to Detective Superintendent Carlton.

Barry Peter Prudom's criminal record dated to 1961 and covered minor crimes such as theft, house-breaking, shop-breaking and taking motor vehicles without consent. He was then wanted for the wounding offence in Leeds, and for dishonestly abstracting electricity at Beverley. He was 5' 9'' tall, of proportionate build with brown curly hair, blue eyes, a pale complexion and a somewhat swarthy appearance. He led a nomadic life, occasionally working on oil rigs and even travelling to America, Canada and the Middle East to seek employment and adventure.

He admired the work and bravery of the SAS and he tried to emulate the daring lifestyle of these men by living in the wild and practising survival techniques. He studied these in a book called *No Need to Die – The Real Techniques of*

Survival by Yorkshire survival expert, Eddie McGee (Compton, 1979).

In 1969, he had joined the TA SAS Volunteer 23rd Regiment in Leeds but was rejected as unsuitable. He enjoyed the use of firearms too, spending time shooting at tin cans, and was a physical fitness fanatic. A one-time apprentice electrician, he became self-employed and even bought a grocer's shop in Leeds. Illegitimate by birth, his mother had committed suicide and it seemed this troubled him deeply. But he could not abandon his desire to live in the wild, to go on manoeuvres with the Territorial Army, to attempt to survive against all odds and to avoid all contact with authority ....

As Prudom's current whereabouts were being investigated, either to eliminate him from this enquiry or to confirm his part in it, the reconstruction of the events surrounding PC Haigh's death was arranged. Between 6 a.m. and 9.30 a.m. on Thursday 24 June, some 270 vehicles passed Warren Point. The exercise generated a lot of goodwill and some very positive publicity coupled with snippets of information. It was also used to bolster the public appeal for sightings of Mr Luckett's stolen 2.6 Rover VAU 875S.

That same day, we were to learn that a brown Rover car bearing the number plates GYG 344T had been seen by a policeman at the Primrose Valley Holiday Village on the Yorkshire coast near Filey; the car was empty at the time, and a check of its registration number showed that it was owned by a company at Pickering in North Yorkshire. That suggested it was innocently parked there.

Under orders not to approach any suspect car alone, the officer left the scene had began to make enquiries about this car because it was a 2.6 litre saloon and the Police National Computer showed that GYG 344T was a 2.3 litre model. It was a minor difference, one which some officers might have overlooked, but then it was learned the real GYG 344T was still in Pickering. The Rover at the Holiday

Village was carrying false number plates. But when suitably prepared officers returned to Primrose Valley, the car had gone. A careful but widespread search was put into immediate effect to trace this suspicious car. No one had seen its driver.

Around 6 p.m. that same evening, Thursday 24 June, PC Ken Oliver of the North Yorkshire Police Dog Section was driving through Bickley Forest which adjoins Dalby Forest on the North York Moors. He was unarmed and alone apart from his police dog and he came across a parked brown Rover. It bore the number GYG 344T but as PC Oliver began to investigate it, and before he had time to release his dog from the rear of his van, a man emerged from the Rover and started to fire at him. He was using a small handgun, either an automatic or semi-automatic, and several shots were fired at the policeman. One grazed his nose, and several others caused him minor injuries as he tried desperately to save his life. His thick uniform helped to ward off the shots to his body and arm, and he found refuge in a nearby cottage with a bullet tear in his uniform.

Miraculously, he was not killed and surprisingly, his assailant did not pursue him, possibly thinking that other officers were nearby, although he did fire at the dog – and missed. He did, however, wreak vengeance upon the parked police van by ripping out the radio, thus denying PC Oliver the opportunity to call for help. Instead of following PC Oliver, the man turned his attention to the parked Rover and set it on fire. As the fire took a hold and the car blazed to destruction, the man vanished into the forest. Within seconds, he had disappeared among thousands of acres of close-growing trees. The late PC Haigh's handcuffs were later found in the ruins of the burnt-out Rover.

But PC Oliver had seen his attacker's face. After he had managed to summon help through some people living in the forest, he was shown a photograph which he identified as his attacker, Barry Peter Prudom, alias Edwards. The police now knew for whom they were seeking, a man who could survive in these wild conditions and who was still carrying a gun.

The police were then faced with the impossible task of searching this huge forest thoroughly, the Dalby portion of which alone covered some twenty-five square miles, about the area of Leeds. They were seeking a man who could kill them before they even saw him, and who could disappear at will among the densely-planted acres. It was a daunting task, and it was made much worse because of the awful weather. Although it was June, there was heavy rain and thick mist, thus reducing visibility to a few yards.

Massive numbers of armed officers would be required to make the slightest impact on this region. But the police had no alternative. A search had to be undertaken and neighbouring forces were asked to supply teams of officers. By first light, four hundred policemen with dogs and guns had been mustered, and RAF helicopters joined the teams as the massive task of organizing a search began. They were helped by gamekeepers and forestry workers who knew the intricate forestry routes, and all holidaymakers were asked to leave the area. Campers, visitors and cottage occupants all left, some not understanding or appreciating the risk they were under, while local forestry workers and residents on lonely farms and smallholdings were all warned of the danger. Some left their homes, but there was concern for those who could not be reached by telephone. It meant a personal visit by a policeman, in itself a tremendous risk.

Road blocks were established at all forestry entrances and exits – this alone required a hundred officers – and so a huge net, albeit with many holes, was established over the forest. It was like seeking the proverbial needle in a haystack, but infinitely more difficult because the needle was moving all the time, and it was also a desperately cunning and dangerous needle. There were times that the public could not understand the immense problems that such a search involved, some believing it entailed little more than searching a small copse or piece of parkland.

It is an area where forestry workers operate in pairs because it is so easy even for an experienced local person to lose his bearings among acres of identical trees upon miles of identical tracks. To sustain a continued presence in the forest, many more officers were needed; already, several police forces were involved in the enquiry, namely North Yorkshire, West Yorkshire, Humberside, Nottinghamshire and Lincolnshire because Prudom had committed crimes in their areas. More men would be required because, unless Prudom was swiftly caught, the searching officers would require rest and refreshment.

But so would Prudom. Could he be flushed out of the forest and if so, where and how? The police presence remained in Dalby and Bickley Forests during that weekend, but there was no sighting. Meanwhile, the evidence against Prudom was such that any court of law would have difficulty in finding him not guilty of at least one of the crimes, and it was decided, because of the exceptional circumstances and the continuing risk to life, to release his photograph, name and description to the press, radio and television, and so to the public. In this way, his image would be imprinted upon the minds of the people and they would know for whom we were all seeking. Hopefully, if Prudom did break cover, someone would recognize him.

I therefore arranged a news conference at Harrogate Police Station for 10 a.m. Monday 28 June during which I would issue the description and photographs of Prudom.

The formal announcement of our suspect's name gave the reporters a welcome fillip for their news coverage after a routine but undramatic weekend, even though Superintendent Carlton stressed that we wanted to speak with him purely for elimination purposes. Dalby Forest and its surroundings were still being searched and an SAS expert said that Prudom could exist there at least for a month by using his basic survival knowledge. It looked like being a long, drawn-out hunt. Things had gone very quiet. Too quiet in fact.

Prudom had slipped through the large-mesh net.

There is every possibility that he followed a stream down from the forest. He would know this would guide him to lower ground and to places of food and shelter. If Prudom followed Thornton Beck from Dalby Forest, it would take him through Thorton-le-Dale to its junction with the River Derwent. By following the path of the Derwent, he would come first to Old Malton, and then to Malton.

And so it was that around 2 p.m. that Monday afternoon, a very dirty, dishevelled and tired-looking old man was seen trudging across some fields on the approach to Old Malton, a pretty village which is a suburb of Malton. Few people paid any attention to him, even though he was wearing a fawn coloured cagoule and had dark, curly hair. He was unshaven too and had a gaunt, thin face with his cheek bones showing through. He carried a shoulder bag or duffle bag of similar colour to his coat and something resembling a radio aerial protruded from this.

According to one witness, he also carried some binoculars and a thumb stick, and wore a blue woolly hat. News of the presence of this man was telephoned to Malton Police Station by a member of the public, one of many such sightings of possible suspects. Two police cars were in the vicinity of Old Malton at the time, one driven by PC Michael Woods and the other by Sergeant David Winter, both unarmed. The cars were ordered to rendezvous in Old Malton and make a search for the tramp-like old man. At 2.15 p.m. they met outside the Post Office at Old Malton to discuss their plans and organize the search.

While they were outside, the 'old man' was inside that

very same Post Office which, like those in so many other villages, also served as a shop. He bought some sausage rolls, a loaf of brown bread and a tin of pilchards and had purchased some sweets from another shop in the village a few minutes earlier. As he left with his purchases, the two police cars were parked outside, just a short distance along the street. PC Woods was seated in his, facing away from the shop, and as the tired figure emerged into the street, Sergeant Winter said, 'I'd better go and check him out.' But as he left his car and approached the tramp, the man pulled a hand gun and the moment Sergeant Winter realized what was happening, he ran for his life. He made for a field opposite the shop and not far from the beautiful old abbey church of St Mary, part of the ancient Gilbertine Priory.

He ran through a gate, but Prudom followed and fired a shot. It hit Sergeant Winter in the neck and he fell; as he lay injured, Prudom shot him a further two times. Deeply shocked, PC Woods went to the aid of his comrade as the killer fled across the fields towards the River Derwent. Ther was nothing he could do to save David Winter; he had died where he had fallen. There were reports of more shots being fired as police cars and officers appeared at the scene within seconds, for Malton Police Station, the focus of the Dalby Forest hunt, was a few hundred yards along the same road. But the elusive Prudom vanished into the lush countryside and the normally peaceful market-town of Malton became a town under siege and the focal point of one of the largest manhunts ever mounted in the United Kingdom.

All available police officers were immediately directed to Malton, and the hunt was concentrated upon a town and not the wild countryside. But Malton is a small town, surrounded on all sides by lush farmland richly covered with woods and thickets, and it was felt that Prudom may attempt to flee to the shelter of the countryside. Immediate steps were therefore taken to seal off all exit routes, a most difficult task even for a town the size of Malton because while roads and rail links may be closed, there were so many other means of escaping on foot to live rough in the hundreds of square miles around the town. The police mounted a 'containment' exercise by which they would keep Prudom within the town limits.

Nonetheless, the huge tract of countryside around Malton had to be meticulously searched and supervised so that if he did succeed in leaving the shelter of the town, he would be flushed out. One danger within the minds of the police was that he might enter a house in the town and take a hostage. We dared not emphasize this publicly in case we planted the idea in Prudom's mind – we believed he was carrying a radio and so listening to all BBC and IRN news bulletins. We sought and won the co-operation of the media on this aspect. The massive publicity already generated was sufficient to persuade the townspeople, and those living in the surrounding countryside, to lock their doors and windows, to safeguard their motor vehicles and not to approach any strangers.

The Chief Constable of North Yorkshire, Mr Kenneth Henshaw, now assumed command of this operation and the shoppers and townspeople of Malton were suddenly swamped by police-officers, some of whom were armed. All roads out of the town were manned at road-blocks, rail and bus stations were monitored and the entire area was quartered on detailed maps so that every portion could be searched. No part of the town would be overlooked and we knew the public would report anything or anyone remotely suspicious. Indeed, throughout the entire hunt, the public response and co-operation was of the highest order.

As Prudom went to ground, the Chief Constable said,

Under no circumstances should anyone approach this man. He is a dangerous, ruthless, callous individual who will not hesitate to shoot at anyone. Anyone who approaches him is in extreme danger of being killed; he is obviously a trained marksman.

With a quarry of this kind, extreme care had to be taken and North Yorkshire Police sought for, and were granted, assistance from neighbouring police areas. By the following day, more than eight hundred police officers from eleven police forces were at Malton and being deployed upon this harrowing and dangerous search. It is worthy of record at this stage to say that in spite of reports of huge numbers of police officers being armed, only some two per cent carried guns, that is about sixteen. The rest carried out this search without arms, an extremely brave commitment to their duty. The town was in a state of continuing terror with constant sightings of Prudom being reported, some of which were genuine. Through the press, radio and television, the police and Prudom's girlfriend asked him to surrender before there was further bloodshed, but he did not respond.

On Wednesday 30 June, with no trace of Prudom, assistance was offered to the police from a most unexpected and interesting quarter. Mr Eddie McGee, the world-renowned survival expert and author of the very book from which Prudom had earlier learned his survival skills, came to Malton and volunteered to join the search.

Mr McGee was a trained commando, a parachutist, an expert in karate, judo and aikido and other forms of self-defence, a knife-thrower, survival expert and businessman. He had learned tracking skills from native tribesmen in places like Borneo, Zaire, the Yemen and the Sahara and had spent some time living with pygmies and learning their skills. He ran an adventure and survival school in the Yorkshire Dales. As his son, himself a policeman said, 'From a set of footprints, he can tell the sex of the person who made them, their size, whether they were carrying anything, whether the load was on their back or front, whether they were injured, how fast they were going and how many minutes ahead they were. He can even tell if a person is sweating or whether they know they are being tracked.'

His special and unique knowledge would be of great assistance, but although of value, this offer did present problems. While Eddie could be the first to locate Prudom, he could not be allowed to carry a firearm, he could not be insured by the police in this dangerous mission nor could the police be held responsible if he was killed or injured. The sole fact that he was a civilian and not a police officer added grave dimensions to his proposed role if he was hurt, but Eddie McGee was aware of all these problems. And he insisted he could help on a voluntary basis and that he could cope with any problem that arose, especially his own safety.

In fact, no finer expert could possibly be found, and so the Chief Constable accepted Mr McGee's offer of help. He would work with a team of eight police officers who were armed. As sightings were reported, therefore, Eddie McGee went to the locations to determine whether or not the marks left behind could have been made by Prudom. There were many false alarms, but some were genuine. From Eddie McGee's reading of these marks, we knew that Prudom had been contained within a five-mile radius of the town. However, he was always on the move and tiring fast, becoming increasingly desperate for food and rest. The master tracker and survival expert was now teaching his pupil a tough lesson. At one stage on the following Friday, he was only some three hours behind Prudom and the search continued all night. Positive sightings of Prudom were made at Huttons Ambo and Low Hutton, two villages on the outskirts of Malton and it became evident that he was moving around in circles, an indication to Mr McGee that he was almost on the point of exhaustion. He would probably lie low somewhere.

In direct contrast to Eddie McGee's ancient skills, the London Metropolitan Police loaned their helicopter which was equipped with the latest heat detection devices and night-sight capabilities. It was hoped this would detect anyone lying concealed in the vegetation around Malton. This was helped by an enormous selection of modern police equipment, vehicles, a computer, and backed up by mobile canteens, sleeping accommodation and police welfare services.

But with all this skill and equipment at the disposal of the police, Prudom evaded capture. Eddie McGee discovered that he was following the disused railway line to make forays into and out of the town while the police were elsewhere. It seemed he was watching their movements and moving only when it was safe to do so, knowing that if he fired at them, he would betray his own position. There can be little doubt that Prudom knew that he was being sought by his hero, who was also one of the world's leading trackers, for he laid false trails to throw him off the scent. These were not successful and Prudom was kept on the move, a fact later borne out by the terrible state of his feet.

By that weekend, Saturday 3 July, Prudom had not been caught. By now, we were convinced that he was still in the town because there had been no sightings in the countryside, no vehicles had been stolen and no reports of houses being broken into or food being stolen. This view was supported by Eddie McGee. By now, he seemed to have vanished, for the trails, both on the ground and by sightings from the public, had ended. He was lying low.

We were later to discover where this was. At teatime on the evening of Saturday 3 July, Mrs Bessie Johnson who lived at The Mount, Malton, a few hundred yards from the police station, was clearing the pots from the table when she found a man hiding behind a chair in her dining-room. He had entered the house while the door was open as they cleared the table, and said, 'You know who I am, don't you?'

At gunpoint, he located Mr Maurice Johnson in the house, then tied up both Mr and Mrs Johnson who were in their seventies. Having watched the house from an outbuilding, he knew that their son Brian would soon be home from work, and when Brian entered, he too was held hostage. Upon seeing his parents held in this way, Brian ran *into* the house. Prudom told him, 'You did the right thing; if you'd run the other way, you'd have had a bullet in your head.'

And so, unknown to anyone, the Johnsons were held hostage at gunpoint for almost eleven hours. Their door was locked and Prudom occupied his time by bathing his torn, blistered and bleeding feet while eating and resting. The family won his confidence and he treated them with sympathy and care, even calling Mr Johnson 'Dad'. But he had no intention of staying – he wanted to kill some more policemen, and so at 3 a.m. on Sunday morning, under cover of darkness, he decided to leave and make his way to the nearby police station where hundreds of policemen and women were coming and going. He mentioned his intention to the Johnsons, adding that he would not be taken alive, and requesting them to give him a full day's start. At 3 a.m., he limped out of their house and slowly moved towards the police station whose lights made it so clearly visible.

Just before 5 a.m. Mr Johnson managed to free himself, and the family made a pretence of going to bed by switching on the upstairs lights in case Prudom was watching their house. In fact Mr Johnson rang Malton Police Station.

Barry Prudom did not reach Malton Police Station. After covering only a few dozen yards, he found himself at the Malton Tennis Courts and Bowling Green, and it may be that sheer exhaustion overcame him for he lay down to shelter in a derelict shed behind a wall and covered himself with a blue plastic sheeting. Whether he went to sleep or not will never be known, but at 5.30 a.m., the police and Eddie McGee were already on the trail. And after a search involving the utmost care, they found him.

It was now almost nine o'clock, with Eddie's every move being protected by three armed police officers. Those officers now contained Prudom in his lair. Repeated calls were made for Prudom to surrender himself to the police, but he refused. Two stun grenades, noisy but largely ineffective in the open, were used in an attempt to frighten him into submission, but he steadfastly refused. Three shots were fired by Prudom. Two were aimed at the police, neither of which hit their targets, and one was returned by a police officer, but it was too late.

Prudom's third shot had entered his own head and, as the pathologist later discovered, that shot killed him. In that dramatic way, the hunt ended and within hours, Malton was, on the surface, returning to normal. It will take years for the memories to be erased, but Malton and district can be justifiably proud of its people, its police force and those who died at Prudom's hands.

We must not forget the tragic events at the home of Mr and Mrs Luckett or the ordeals of PCs Ken Oliver and Mick Woods. In those awful weeks, they were all magnificent.

But two mysteries surround Prudom's murderous behaviour. One relates to the number plates he used on the brown Rover car which he stole from the Lucketts. It is still not known where he obtained those and how he managed to select a registration number which belonged to a car of the same make and colour as the one he was using, but which was also owned by a firm in the area where he was then operating. The chances of that being a coincidence are astronomical.

The second puzzle is why he embarked on that terrible act of destruction which caused so much distress to innocent families.

That will remain one of our criminal mysteries.

Another unusual aspect of this case is worthy of note. When, moments before he was murdered, PC David Haigh wrote down Prudom's date of birth and the registration number of his Citroën car, he effectively detected his own murder.

11 The Unknown Lady of Sutton Bank

Sutton Bank lies upon the A170 as one leaves Thirsk and heads towards Scarborough. Some five miles out of Thirsk, this famous hill snakes up Whitestone Cliff as a twisting climb which extends for about one mile in three steep gradients, 20% (1-in-5), 25% (1-in-4) and again 20% (1-in-5). The steep road presents no worries to local motorists but it does cause immense problems to drivers who are unfamiliar with such a long, twisting ascent. It is especially worrying to those who attempt to drive up these gradients while towing trailers such as boats or caravans, or attempting the climb in heavily-laden lorries and coaches. Happily, in 1984, caravans were forbidden to use this stretch of the A170 which means that local drivers can hopefully have a clear passage up 'their' bank.

From the summit there is one of England's finest views and probably the best in the whole of Yorkshire. The vista is truly breathtaking and extends towards the distant Pennines across the Yorkshire Dales, then over to Teesside in the north and down into West Yorkshire and beyond in the south. For centuries, this view has attracted visitors and sightseers, while the hilltop tracks carried an ancient route and a drovers' road from Scotland into England.

It was here, in 1138, that Gundred the Bountiful of Thirsk, mother of the landowner Roger de Mowbray, gave to some wandering monks a piece of land near Hood Hill.

The hill, which stands just below Sutton Bank, was said

to have been a place of human sacrifice in pagan times, but she allowed the monks to settle here. These were the monks who later built the nearby Byland Abbey.

It was to this point in 1322 that Robert Bruce led the Scots to battle against the English at nearby Scots Corner, a few hundred yards from Sutton Bank Top. This Scots Corner should not be confused with Scotch Corner on the A1. The fight became known as the Battle of Byland, and the English were well and truly beaten; their King, Edward II, fled to the protection of Byland Abbey in the valley below but left for York just before the Scots raided it, sacked it and stole the King's jewels. They then turned their attention to nearby Rievaulx Abbey.

Other famous people who came this way included John Wesley who passed through in March 1755, and William Wordsworth who admired the view in July 1802. He came with his sister Dorothy and paused here on his journey to Brompton near Scarborough where he was to be married. After his wedding in October the same year, and now accompanied by his new wife, Mary (née Hutchinson), he paused once again, this time at dusk, before going on to Thirsk. He wrote a sonnet about the view in which he mentioned an 'Indian citadel, Temple of Greece and Minster with its tower, substantially expressed.' Dorothy, in her journal, also mentions 'a minster unusually distinct, minerets in another quarter and a round Grecian temple.'

The Minster is clearly that of York, but identification of those other points will cause the viewer a good deal of puzzlement.

Tucked into the woodland below Sutton Bank Top is the silvery water of Lake Gormire. There is a steep but delightful walk and a nature trail leading down to the lakeside. This tarn-like lake is about one-third of a mile in circumference and it is remarkable because no streams run into or out of it. It is a natural lake which is rich with wildlife and it probably dates from glacial times. The mystery of its formation has given rise to some legends –

one says the lake is bottomless and another claims that it conceals an entire village, complete with church and spire. The Devil is also linked to the lake. One story says that he leapt from the cliff behind while astride a white horse, and crashed to earth to form the crater which then filled with water. Another legend says that a white mare carrying a girl leapt to its death over the cliff behind Gormire, and that the body of the girl was never found.

The pale cliff in question is known as White Mare Crag and one theory is that the name comes from the white or silvery surface of the lake, i.e. White Mere Crag. This 'white mare' link has no connection with a huge White Horse carved into the hillside about a mile to the south. This is the famous White Horse of Kilburn, carved here in 1857 by the people and schoolchildren of that village. It is now a landmark and can be seen from as far as seventy miles.

In the valley below is the derelict Nevison House, once the home of the notorious seventeenth-century highwayman, William Nevison. He was nicknamed 'Swift Nick' by no less a person than Charles II, and lore says it was he rode the famous Black Bess from London to York, not Dick Turpin.

On the top of Sutton Bank there is much of interest. Near the huge car-park, the National Park Information Centre contains a wealth of detail about the entire district, and especially Sutton Bank and other parts of the North York Moors National Park. There is a stunning cliff-top walk around the edge of the Yorkshire Gliding Club's airfield to the White Horse of Kilburn, and the long-distance footpath, the Cleveland Way, passes through here.

Half a mile or so from the top of the bank is the Hambleton Hotel behind which broad plains stretch towards the distant moors. These continue to serve as gallops for racehorses, and this was the location of the legendary Black Hambleton Races between 1715 and 1770.

The turf here is said to be the best in England for training racehorses and strings of them at exercise are still a regular sight.

The ancient drovers' road passed this way too, joining what is now the A170 close to the Hambleton Hotel. It ran from Scotland to enter the North York Moors near Swainby, then pass along the heights of Black Hambleton as it approached Sutton Bank Top. The drovers' road forked here, with one route decending into upper Ryedale near Oldstead and going on to Coxwold and York.

The other turned along what is now the route of the A170, but bore right at Tom Smith's Cross where a high-wayman of that name was gibbeted. It led along what is still known as Ampleforth High Street (the route of a Roman highway, albeit a long way out of that village), then via Oswaldkirk Bank Top and Hovingham into Malton.

Although cattle-droving had been practised since medie-val times, it reached its peak in the eighteenth and nine-teenth centuries. To feed London's rapidly-increasing population, hundreds of thousands of cattle were required and so they were driven on foot from Scotland and the north, to be sold at local markets. Some of the processions were two miles long. On the road's fifteen-mile stretch across this part of the North York Moors, there were four halts, all inns. Parts of that ancient track continue to serve as a road, but only one halt remains as an inn – the Hambleton Hotel at Sutton Bank Top.

Fairly recently, Sutton Bank Top featured in a national celebration. A massive bonfire was lit nearby on 6 June 1977 to commemorate the Silver Jubilee of Her Majesty Queen Elizabeth II. It was No.82 in a chain of 103 fires stretching from Jersey in the Channel Isles to Saxavord in the Shet-lands. The first fire was lit at Windsor Castle and I was present when the Sutton Bank fire was lit twenty minutes later.

Sutton Bank is certainly a place of history and legend and I was involved in two mysteries at this place.

The first is a ghost story dating to the reign of James I, and the second concerns the body of a woman found in 1981. She has never been identified.

With reference to the ghost story, I write a regular Countryman's Diary for the *Darlington and Stockton Times* under my pseudonym of Nicholas Rhea. In January 1980, I received a call from a motorist who had been driving late at night along the A170 near Sutton Bank Top. He had seen the figure of a woman in seventeenth-century dress dart across the road and into the forest beside the road, after apparently begging a lift or seeking help. So concerned was he for her safety, that he halted to make a search for her. She had been dressed in dark clothing, but he never found her and later heard that he might have seen a ghost. He wrote to me and I mentioned his sighting in my column.

As a result, I was informed that this could have been the ghost of Abigail Glaister. Abigail lived at Kilburn, not far from Sutton Bank Top, and during the reign of James I, she was suspected of being a witch. She was pursued by men and hounds who wanted to capture her for execution, but she leapt over Whitestone Cliff near Lake Gormire and was killed. Since that time, her ghost has been seen many times near Sutton Bank Top, often seeking help from passers-by.

Upon mentioning this, I received a letter from a lady who lives near Northallerton. When towing their caravan over Sutton Bank Top late one night, she and her husband saw the figure of a woman apparently begging a lift.

She was dressed all in black, but when they pulled up to give her a lift, she vanished. Friends following in another car also saw the lady in black and together, they made a search of the area, but found nothing. Recorded sightings of this ghost and its probable identity have been published regularly and it is just another of the long list of legends and mysteries which can be linked to this famous Yorkshire beauty spot.

But surely the most fascinating and puzzling is the identity of the mysterious woman whose body was found close to Sutton Bank Top in August 1981. The most exhaustive, skilled and prolonged enquiries have failed to identify her.

The story began on Friday 28 August 1981 at 8 a.m. A man telephoned Ripon Police Station and said that there was a decomposed body beside the minor road to Scawton and Rievaulx Abbey, not far from its junction with the A170 Thirsk-Scarborough Road. In a well-spoken voice, with perhaps just a trace of a local accent, he gave precise instructions on how to find the body, saying it lay among weeds on the left of the road as one drives to Scawton, and added that it was very close to the entrance to Scawton Moor House Farm.

When the duty police officer asked for his name and address, the man declined and gave the curious response, 'I can't identify myself for reasons of national security.'

At first, these words suggested a crank call and it seemed rather odd that anyone would ring Ripon Police Station with this information, because Thirsk is by far the nearest. But it was then realized that Thirsk Police Station was not manned at that time for the entire twenty-four hours. Any telephone calls to Thirsk Police Station when it was unmanned were automatically diverted to Ripon. And so it was felt that the caller had intended to ring Thirsk with his news.

The local village constable, who knew the area intimately, was directed to investigate this strange, anonymous report. When he arrived, he found no obvious sign of a body, but then began a more meticulous search. Eventually, after a great deal of patience and skill, he found what appeared to be one or two pieces of slender, well-weathered wood deep beneath a huge bed of rosebay willow herbs. These were barely recognizable as human bones, but the sparse remains of a skull convinced him that he had found the body. He called in the CID and the

Scenes of Crimes experts for what was clearly going to be a very difficult investigation. Even at this stage, it was highly improbable that anyone could have stumbled across the remains and recognized them as human. Even the most observant of people could have walked across them and never known them as human remains. So did the caller know they were there before he claimed to have 'found' them? Indeed, had he placed the body there? It seemed that the caller knew far more than he was prepared to admit.

Led by Detective Chief Superintendent Strickland Carter of North Yorkshire Police CID, a team of detectives visited the scene. The remains of the skeleton were most difficult to locate and examine. At the entrance to Scawton Moor House Farm, there is a small concrete hardstanding once used for accommodating milk churns as they awaited collection by milk lorries.

From that point and running for several hundred yards along the wide verge of this narrow lane, is a huge bed of rosebay willow herbs. In August, they are well over six feet high and they grow so densely that one cannot see between their stems. At the base, the thick growth, over the years, has obliterated everything on the ground. Immediately behind the rosebay willow herbs is a close-growing plantation of coniferous trees, while between them and the willow herbs is a low, almost ruined, dry-stone wall.

The area near the concrete hardstanding was often used by families as a parking place for picnics, and so the verge immediately surrounding it was devoid of willow herbs. Children would play here and parents would sit outside their cars enjoying the moorland breezes, the scent of the conifers and the sunshine. And less than five feet away from them, lay the unidentified body. It was lying almost parallel with the dry-stone wall, only some two feet away from it.

It was evident from the beginning that the body had

been there for a considerable time, but nonetheless, the customary caution and attention to detail was never abandoned. Detective Chief Superintendent Carter and his team began a very methodical investigation of the scene, eventually clearing a huge area of willow herbs so that the ground, and the bones, could be more closely examined. Every tiny object was labelled and retained, and Dr Michael Green, the Forensic Pathologist from the University of Leeds Department of Forensic Medicine was called in to examine the body in the position in which it lay.

My part in this enquiry was that of the press officer, my task was to create the necessary publicity which might help in identifying the body and solving the crime, if indeed a crime had been committed. That a crime had been committed was by no means certain. I arrived at the same time as Dr Green and watched him carry out his fascinating forensic investigation. By this time – around 4.30 p.m. – the entire width of willow herbs had been removed and the scene had been examined and photographed, with all the found objects listed and preserved for scientific investigation.

The meagre remains of the body were now exposed, but even now could barely be recognized as human. But they did provide a lot of information for Dr Green. The surviving pelvic bone told him that these were the remains of a woman while the residue and insect larvae which had bred within the skull told him she had lain here for about two years.

Having completed his on-site examination of the body, Dr Green took the remains to his laboratory for a more detailed examination, and officers of the Task Force then began a fingertip search of the scene and surrounding area. I felt it might be prudent to withhold publicity of this discovery until later that evening. If we did not announce the discovery on the evening television and radio bulletins, we felt that the anonymous caller would wonder whether his call had been taken seriously and might be tempted to return to the scene to see if his telephone call had produced any positive police action. And so, for those exceptional reasons, I did not announce the finding of the body until all the regional evening news bulletins had been broadcast. Surely a lack of news about the body would prompt the caller to take further action? Maybe he would make another telephone call? Officers were concealed in the nearby woods to record any visits to the scene and although their all-night woodland vigil did, from within those forests, produce some startling results from the world of illicit love affairs, it did not produce a suspect. At nine o'clock, therefore, I informed the Press Association of the discovery and the publicity was thus set in motion.

In the meantime, the microscopic examination of the verge by the Task Force had produced results. The lid of a jar of meat-paste was found directly beneath where the body had lain, and later, some two inches into the ground, they found a solitary toe-nail, painted red.

On the low dry-stone wall immediately behind the body, and less than two feet away from it, the Task Force found a cardboard box containing six empty wine bottles. One of them had contained Carbonnieux red wine bottled on 3 October 1980. Whoever placed that box on the wall must have stepped over the body. We appealed for that person to come forward, but our appeals produced no one; by that time, the body had lain there for one year and could by then have been decomposed and the bones concealed, even at close range.

Examination of the meat-paste lid showed that the contents of the jar had been sold by the manufacturers on 6 October 1979, and it was probably discarded shortly afterwards by someone having a picnic. The red varnish on the toe-nail was identified as being a Max Factor cosmetic of the Maxi range. The date of the lid told us that the body had been placed there *after* 6 October 1979, while the insect larvae told us she had lain there for about two years. So it seemed she had been placed among the rosebay willow herbs sometime during the autumn of 1979. This date was later confirmed by a jockey who daily exercised racehorses; every day, he rode past the body's resting-place, and during the October of 1979, he had become aware of an awful smell which emanated from among the willow herbs. He thought it might be the rotting carcase of a fox, dog or larger animal, and after two or three days, felt he should investigate its source.

But having made that decision, he fell off his horse and broke a leg; he was in hospital for a few weeks and upon his discharge, the smell had gone. He did not carry out his investigation, but could pinpoint the date because he kept a diary of events.

As the police began their search of all records of missing women, both locally and nationally, Dr Green's analysis of the few bones produced a surprising amount of information. He could say that she was an adult, around 38-40 years of age and about 5′ 2″ tall. She was very slender and had had natural dark brown hair, cut to a length of about four or six inches. A few strands still adhered to the skull, but most of the other bones of the body had been carried away, probably by wild animals.

She had borne children, probably three but certainly two, and she had an abnormality of her spine which would have caused backache at some stage of her life. She took size 4 shoes and, as already noted, used Max Factor pink nail varnish on her toes. She had false teeth in her upper jaw, and six natural teeth in her lower jaw, these being stained, probably by nicotine.

Later examination of her teeth by the Dental School of Newcastle University confirmed the age of the woman, but suggested she had neglected the hygiene of her mouth and teeth. We did learn, however, that her formative years, until about the age of seven, had been spent in an area with a high degree of natural fluoride in the drinking water.

Two local areas which qualified in that respect were the towns of Hartlepool and Grimsby, and this prompted detailed enquiries in those towns, particularly to trace any missing women.

It was also noted that the body had been completely naked, with no item or remnants of any clothing being found upon or near the body, nor had we found any jewellery, watch, rings or other adornment. This suggested the body had been placed there with a deliberate purpose of concealing it and it had been done in such a manner that identification would be difficult, if not impossible. The cause of her death was never revealed to the press or the public, although we did announce that the death was, for obvious reasons, 'suspicious.' It was stated she had met her death by unnatural causes, and so a murder-type investigation was launched.

The nation's registers of missing women were scanned and assistance was given by a whole range of sources, both official and unofficial, through which a woman's absence might be noticed. Children's homes were contacted in the hope that some children might have missed recent visits by their mother, and the public was asked to report the absence of any single woman who may have been a friend, neighbour or work colleague. Employers were asked to check their registers and teams of detectives contacted all the local places where such a woman might have been employed or might have been missed.

One aspect affecting this locality was the number of holidaymakers who came here; caravans, campers, bed-and-breakfast establishments, hotels and boarding-houses were all considered, and all proprietors were asked to check their registers in the hope it might jog a distant memory. Motorists were asked to recall if they had given a lift to a lone woman, while the Salvation Army's records, hostels for the homeless and the various welfare organizations were asked to scan their records for missing women who might fit the vague description of the lady at Sutton Bank Top. Dentists were provided with details of the woman's teeth in the hope someone might recognize his or her own workmanship, especially upon her false teeth. All this produced nothing.

And then we turned up something dramatic and exciting. At about the time we believed the body had been placed beside that road, we learned that a woman prisoner from Askham Grange Open Prison near York had escaped. She had been sentenced to a term of imprisonment for manslaughter. She had fled more than two years ago and had never been seen since. When her physical description was examined, it was found that it matched that of the Sutton Bank body in six respects. Age, height, colour of hair and build were similar; she had had children and more amazingly, she had had trouble with her back. It seemed we had found a name for our corpse.

But with such scant relics to work on, how could this be proved?

The only way was to find the escaped prisoner; she had been absent now for some two years and it was highly unlikely that she would voluntarily come forward for elimination. To do so could result in her being taken straight back to prison. One added problem was that she had come originally from Eire, and enquiries there had failed to trace her.

With the consent of the Home Office, therefore, we decided to publicize this new line of enquiry, and I got the task of alerting newspapers, TV and radio stations, particularly those in Eire and Northern Ireland. We issued a plea to the prisoner that, if she was still alive, she should obtain a piece of white paper and imprint it with her fingerprints. Having been subjected to the police arrest procedure, she knew how to do this. She should then send those prints to Detective Chief Superintendent Carter at the North Yorkshire Police Headquarters. He would be able to compare them with her criminal record, and thus confirm that she was alive. We stressed, however, that this course of action and any assistance she might give, could in no way absolve her from any future legal action.

It must be said that none of us expected a response; if she was still alive, what finer cover could she hope for than for everyone to assume she was dead? Was it likely she would blow her own cover to assist the police in this enquiry? Would she risk capture and the possibility of a return to prison?

She did. Shortly after our appeal, Mr Carter received two neat pieces of white paper, each bearing fingerprints and accompanied by a friendly little note. When these were compared with her criminal record, it proved she was still alive and now we knew she was living somewhere in Eire. She had blown the perfect cover, and we had still not identified the lady. And that prisoner continued to evade capture.

It was inevitable that a widely publicized enquiry of this nature would attract cranks; we received lots of time-wasting calls and letters from those odd people who insist on providing dubious help and advice, or even confessing to the 'crime.' One crank wrote to claim he knew the killer's name, the woman's name and the identity of our anonymous caller. He said that Superintendent John Carlton, Mr Carter's deputy, had to broadcast on Radio Hallam, Sheffield, using a code supplied by the writer, when all would be revealed. Mr Carlton did this, but no one contacted us with the correct information; the writer was traced and eliminated from the enquiry. It was a time-wasting exercise but one which had to be undertaken just in case it proved genuine.

A clairvoyant then claimed to link this corpse with that of a man found in West Yorkshire the same day, the link being the figure A170. This was the road near which our body was found but our enquiries showed that there was no possible link between that man and our dead lady.

Oddly enough, however, the father of that West

Yorkshire victim did regularly drive along the A170, right past the scene of our discovery.

These were just some examples of dozens of false trails that were presented to the investigating teams, and their hopes were lifted soon afterwards by the discovery of a woman's clothes in a wood only a mile from the scene. These comprised a black evening gown, a bra and some pants; they were hanging from a tree, but we could not link them with the dead woman. No one came forward to claim them. Then a macabre touch of humour occurred during our searches of the scene – as the Task Force conducted their patient search of the woods nearby, a hearse arrived, complete with plastic flowers and a coffin. It was accompanied by a film crew, and was part of a sequence for Thora Hirds' TV comedy series *In Loving Memory*. We felt that neither party knew of the other's presence.

By November that year, it seemed that all possible avenues of enquiry had been exhausted; the records of several hundred missing women had been examined without success and it seemed there was nothing further that could be done. Then Chief Superintendent Carter announced a unique development.

Experts from the Department of Medical Illustration at Manchester University had studied the remains of the skull and had measured it.

They felt it would be possible to construct a life-size model of the woman's head, by adding wax to a replica of her skull so that realistic features would be reproduced. Although there could be no guarantee of accuracy, it was felt this might produce a passable image of what she had looked like in life, and so the model was made.

The make up was done by the staff of Granada Television and a news conference was arranged so that photographs of the model head would be widely circulated in the newspapers and on television. It was a macabre sight; the life-size head was complemented by short, dark brown hair and brown eyes set in a natural flesh-coloured face of considerable character. So far as we knew, this was the first time such a model had been used by the British Police in an attempt to identify a body.

The publicity prompted callers to provide several more names and some new lines of enquiry, but in spite of everyone's efforts, it did not achieve a positive identification.

And that is the present situation.

After years of investigation, the name of the mystery lady of Sutton Bank Top remains unknown. The identity of the mystery caller and his role is also unknown, but the police continue to search their files in the hope that, one day, the name of a missing woman will match the remains found on the morning of 28 August 1981 near Sutton Bank Top, one of Yorkshire's finest beauty spots.

Index